LEAVING RELIGION, FOLLOWING JESUS

Smyth & Helwys Publishing, Inc.
6316 Peake Road
Macon, Georgia 31210-3960
1-800-747-3016

Printed in the United States of America.

The paper used in this publication meets the minimum requirements of
American National Standard for Information Sciences—
Permanence of Paper for Printed Library Materials.
ANSI Z39.48–1984. (alk. paper)

Library of Congress Cataloging-in-Publication Data

McBrayer, Ronnie.

Leaving religion, following Jesus / by Ronnie McBrayer.
p. cm. Includes bibliographical references.
ISBN 978-1-57312-531-4 (pbk. : alk. paper)
1. Christian life. I. Title. BV4501.3.M324 2009 248.4—dc22
2009010526

Leaving Religion, FOLLOWING JESUS

RONNIE McBRAYER

Also by Ronnie McBrayer

But God Meant It for Good
Lessons From the Life of Joseph

Keeping the Faith
Passages, Proverbs, Parables

Dedication

For Jether Cochran

Acknowledgments

If gratitude is the memory of the heart, then I have more memories than I can count.

First, to the hardworking staff at Smyth & Helwys—thank you. Especially Keith Gammons and my editor Leslie Andres who always pulls off the hat trick of being supportive, exacting, and thorough. Again, thank you.

To the people of A Simple Faith who gather in Santa Rosa Beach, Florida, and via the web: You have given me far more than I can ever offer in return. Your encouragement and eagerness to follow Christ inspires me daily. You are in my heart.

To my closest friends who have helped me incubate and process the words in this book: Chris, Bala and Joni, Sean, Billy, and Chad. You are all as close as family; just without so much of the baggage. Thank you.

And to my wife, Cindy, for whom I am most grateful: You are God's gracious gift to me, and I would be just about helpless without you. Thank you, and the boys—Blayze, Bryce, and Braden—for allowing me long hours in front of the computer screen. You are all fiercely and forever loved.

Contents

Introduction

> No one can know Christ unless he follows after him in life.
>
> —Hans Denk

I have no idea what it is like to be followed by disciples on a journey to Jerusalem. I do, however, know what it is like to take three young children across the country. It can't be much different. Like the proverbial herding of cats.

Recently my wife and I took our three sons on an epic journey that we had planned for more than a year. It was also a journey I anticipated since the birth of my first son more than a decade ago. Having traveled through a great deal of the American West myself, I wanted nothing more than to reach the day when my children could see and experience it for themselves. Now that they were all in elementary school, it seemed like the right time to fill their vista with the shapes, colors, and diversity of Arizona's desert. I knew the sight would blow them away, just as it does me.

For a week we rambled like eager disciples along the highways, railways, and airways of the Southwest taking in the majesty of it all. It was fantastic, but not quite as grand as I had hoped. My children buried their heads in electronic games and stuffed their ears with headphones most of the time and missed out on some of the greatest wonders of the world. They may not have missed the wonder of it all, but they failed to soak it up. I had to spend a great deal of time redirecting their attention. Repeatedly I told them, "Our time here is short, so put your toys away. Look around you. Open your eyes. You may never pass this way again."

My boys are probably no different than most of us. We set out on our journeys but hardly lift our heads or open our ears to the wonder around us. We let the time pass, the miles click by, obsessed with lesser things while the glory of a greater world surrounds us.

This is not a book about gaining more knowledge about Jesus. It is not a book, in spite of its title, about tearing down or criticizing religious institutions. I did not write it to give you facts about a rebellious first-century rabbi.

This is a book about running after Jesus, about a journey with the Christ—his journey and yours. It is a book about looking and listening to the unexpected. It is a book about opening our eyes, unstopping our ears, and soaking up the gracious wonder that he is, the wonder that surrounds us.

So put away your toys and follow Jesus. Look at him and listen. Open your eyes. Take it all in. We may never pass this way again.

Ronnie McBrayer
Freeport, Florida

Chapter 1

A Hazardous Journey

> Men wanted for hazardous journey. Small wages, bitter cold, long months of complete darkness, constant danger, safe return doubtful.
>
> —Ernest Shackleton

Jour-ney \ *ˋjər-nē* \: an act or instance of traveling from one place to another.

When was the last time you took a journey? Was it a long-awaited vacation? A ride to the beach? A wait-in-line, empty-your-pockets, remove-your-shoes pass through airport security on assigned business? An outing to the bookstore where now you hold this book in your hand?

We take many journeys, and it has always been so, for we are roving, migrating animals. Scientists say that our genetic ancestors began their journey out of Africa tens of thousands of years ago. That journey has continued throughout our history, circled our planet, and now ventures beyond it. Humans are always crawling toward the edge, toward the margin, toward the unknown to see what lies around the corner or over the next hill. To journey, even into danger—often especially into danger—is programmed into our DNA.

Consider a few of the more important journeys that have defined our lives. In 1492 Christopher Columbus traveled across the Atlantic and "discovered" the new world. In truth, he accidentally stumbled upon the Western Hemisphere. As the old joke goes, "When he left, Columbus didn't know where he was going; when he got here he didn't know where he was; and when he returned he didn't know where he had been." That sounds like more than one family vacation I have taken.

Then there is the famed expedition of Lewis and Clark that opened up the American West. The men and women of that expedition took so many steps that they wore out a pair of moccasins every other day, needing some four hundred pairs to get back home.

For those of us who can fly to most any location in the world at a moment's notice, we might forget the heroic flight of Charles Lindbergh, who made the first nonstop trans-Atlantic flight in his *Spirit of St. Louis* only eight decades ago. It took him more than thirty hours, but then, a single generation later, a technological leap put a man on the moon.

When Neil Armstrong stepped off the *Apollo 11* landing craft onto the lunar surface, he said, "That's one small step for a man, one giant leap for mankind." This is what humans have always done. With small, sometimes unsteady steps, we have journeyed on.

Journeys have determined your own life. You traveled through childhood, adolescence, and somehow survived middle school. One day you journeyed across a stage and received a diploma. You may have taken faltering steps down an aisle to where a groom and a preacher waited for you, or stood at the altar and watched your bride approach. There is the frantic, nerve-racking journey from home in the middle of the night as you go to the hospital to deliver your child, and there in the delivery room another journey begins for yet another human being.

We travel into middle age—the journey that takes us over the hill; the journey that leads to retirement; and the journey that takes us to the next life, to that "undiscovered country, from whose bourn no traveler returns."[1]

The Christian faith tradition is filled with journeys. Father Abraham left family and familiar territory and headed out like Columbus or Armstrong to an unknown world that only God could reveal. The children of Israel, delivered from slavery, made a forty-year journey across the Sinai Desert, like bickering children trapped in the family station wagon, fighting all the way to the promised land.

Moses took the journey up the mountain to receive the word of God. Mary and Joseph journeyed through field and fountain, moor and mountain to Bethlehem. Jesus traveled up the hill to the cross. The disciples, running like lunatics, made their journey to an empty tomb. Paul, who had the traveling bug more than most, traversed Europe, Asia, and Africa on his journey sharing the gospel. Today, we find ourselves on a journey, looking for a city whose founder and maker is God.

I want you to consider one more journey that perhaps no one has invited you to take. It is a grand expedition found in the heart of the New

Testament Gospels, a journey made by Jesus and his disciples as they traveled together through Judea to Jerusalem.

Matthew ignores this six-month journey. Mark summarizes it in a single verse (Mark 10:1). John, a bit more generous, gives it half a chapter (John 7:1-10). But Luke, always meticulous, novel, and imaginative, gives this journey nine chapters—a full third of his Gospel. Jesus' Great Journey to Jerusalem begins in Luke 9:51 and continues through Luke 18:14. This is a journey worth taking.

Most New Testament scholars contend that the Gospel of Mark was the first to be written down. Matthew and Luke most certainly used Mark, among other written and oral accounts, as a source and guide for their own Gospels. Luke says as much: "Many people have set out to write accounts about the events that have been fulfilled among us. They used the eyewitness reports circulating among us from the early disciples. Having carefully investigated everything from the beginning, I also have decided to write a careful account" (Luke 1:1-3a).

Luke was not an eyewitness to the events he recorded. He became a follower of Christ post-resurrection. So he set out like a reporter or a research historian to gather as many events, stories, and words of Jesus as possible. He must have discovered a lot along the way because he ends up being a wordy kind of guy. His Gospel is the longest of the four (in fact, word for word it is the longest book of the New Testament), and he was the only one to write a sequel. Sequels are rarely as good as the originals, but his, the book of Acts, turned out all right. Take Luke with Acts, as a two-volume set, and Luke has more to say than any other single writer in the New Testament, even the prolific Apostle Paul.

Luke's gathering of the facts, however, did not make him a mechanized android, impartially collecting information and then throwing it out there, saying, "I report, you decide." Instead, Luke weaved an intentional narrative—holy propaganda, I might call it. This is the "Gospel according to Luke." This is the good news as heard and seen by Luke, as told by Luke, and as interpreted by Luke, with a personal, distinct voice. As a believer and a convert to Christ, Luke, like every Christian, has a one-of-a-kind story to tell.

Luke is not interested in providing objective, sterile facts about Jesus, something you might read in an encyclopedia or at Wikipedia.com. For far too long we have read the Gospels this way. Rather, Luke shows us a living, breathing, live and in color Jesus who is more than a man born in Bethlehem who pulled a few rabbits out of his hat and happened to be executed at the hands of the Jewish aristocracy and the Roman Empire. Luke is more concerned that people align themselves with the redemptive purpose of God that Jesus represents.[2] Luke's intention in writing is that people understand who God is through this person of Jesus, and begin to live their lives under Jesus' rule and thus the rule of God.

With fresh, innovative material, Luke finds an unparalleled voice, writing to bring people to his view of Jesus. Nowhere is Luke more intentional or more sharply focused than in the Great Journey. Again, the journey begins in Luke 9, a sort of hinge upon which the book of Luke turns. Chapters 1 through 8 work up to it, and following Luke 9:51, the book moves at incredible speed toward a climax and resolution. This hinge chapter of Luke 9 is jam-packed.

- Luke 9:1-6—Jesus sends out the twelve.
- Luke 9:7-9—Jesus attracts the interest of King Herod and political authorities.
- Luke 9:10-17—Jesus miraculously feeds the five thousand.
- Luke 9:18-27—Peter confesses Jesus as the Christ of God.
- Luke 9:28-47—Jesus is transfigured on the mountainside with Moses and Elijah.

Luke wants us to see that Jesus is at the height of his public ministry. Missionaries are sent out. Public opinion is on the rise. The political powers are beginning to pay attention to him. The disciples, led by Peter, proclaim Jesus as the Messiah. Signs and wonders in the miraculous feeding of the masses confirm his identity. But then Jesus throws a monkey wrench into the works. Note how Luke phrases his words:

> Jesus warned his disciples not to tell anyone who he was. "The Son of Man must suffer many terrible things," he said. "He will be rejected by the elders, the leading priests, and the teachers of religious law. He will be killed, but on the third day he will be raised from the dead." (Luke 9:21-22)

> While everyone was marveling at everything he was doing, Jesus said to his disciples, "Listen to me and remember what I say. The Son of Man is going to be betrayed into the hands of his enemies." But they didn't know what he meant. (Luke 9:43-45)

> As the time drew near for him to ascend to heaven, Jesus resolutely set out for Jerusalem. (Luke 9:51)

> As they were walking along, someone said to Jesus, "I will follow you wherever you go." But Jesus told him, "Anyone who puts a hand to the plow and then looks back is not fit for the kingdom of God." (Luke 9:57, 62)

At the peak of his popularity, Jesus turns to his disciples and says, "Gentlemen, we are leaving all this behind, and we are going to Jerusalem." Jesus gathered his courage and, with a face like flint, he "steeled himself for the journey" before him.[3] Jesus put his hand to his own plow and refused to look back. The Great Journey of Jesus is not linear. Jesus doubled back more than once, made circles and figure eights, and rarely followed the shortest distance between two points. But while his path may have wandered all over the Judean countryside, his purpose and intention remained singularly focused.

Luke gives us a self-aware Jesus who knows this journey is fraught with dangers, who knows the religious and imperial powers of the day will crush him beneath their feet, who knows this journey will cost him his life. Still, he travels resolutely forward to the city that stoned and killed its prophets. He must, for this is his calling, his destiny and vocation: to reveal the identity and true nature of God, even though the world's powers would rather kill that God than live with him.

Of course, the disciples understand none of this. They have their heads buried and their ears shut. "A trip?" they ask in excitement. "We love trips! Oh, and it is a trip to Jerusalem, the capital city. Even better!"

The original band of Jesus followers must have thought this journey was a kind of inauguration. In their minds, Jesus' going to Jerusalem must have meant he was finally going to take charge, to seize King David's throne, to bring to earth the kingdom of God. As Jesus' focus narrowed on the Holy City, they surely felt that they stood on the cusp of all they ever hoped and prayed for, and they figured they would get to be the Messiah's sterling knights seated at the round table of power.

They were clueless that this journey led to a cross. The disciples were so busy picking out the drapes for their new kingly castles that they could not hear what Jesus said directly to them. Only later, with hearts broken, collapsed in a heap along the side of the road, and drowned in tears, did they admit this journey—this Jesus—was not at all what they expected.

Though Jesus warned his disciples often, maybe he did not exactly help them see the big picture. They could not have gotten their minds around it anyway, for if they had understood Jesus' call to radical discipleship, they might have kept fishing, collecting taxes, or tending to their shops and fields. If they had understood what they really faced, they simply would have hit the snooze button, rolled over, and pulled the covers over their heads.

The initial invitation to join Jesus on this journey, as jarring as it was with all the talk of death and unhappy endings, is not the only thing that unsettled those who followed him. Jesus' preferred teaching method—the parable—seemed quaint and harmless at first, but later these stories coiled up like irritated snakes, biting at their listeners. On this Great Journey, more than any other time in his ministry, Jesus uses the parable as his primary and startling means of communication.

There are about three dozen major parables of Jesus. Nineteen are unique to Luke. Imagine Luke going about the work of collecting all the necessary information for his Gospel. There were no archived collections of daily newspapers at the local library. He could not Google "Jesus" and get 185 million hits. (Try it. See how many you get). Written records were scarce. How did Luke gather the accounts he needed? Through personal interviews and conversations. He likely talked to the eyewitnesses who knew, saw, and heard Jesus firsthand. As people began to reminisce about their experiences with this extraordinary man, what did they remember first? Jesus' stories.

"Oh yes, I remember a story Jesus told," they might have said. As much as we are a journeying people, we are also a story-telling people. It should come as no surprise that these two essential human elements join in Jesus' ministry of Luke 9–18.

Again, just as the journey itself sweeps away all expectations, so do Jesus' stories. By telling stories, Jesus isn't somehow putting sugar in a spoon to make the medicine go down a bit easier. These stories *are* the medicine. These stories are an extension and explanation of Jesus' revolutionary ministry. These stories show us that things are not as they appear. Our tidy, well-packaged ideas about spirituality, faith, and reality shatter when confronted by Christ and the God he represents.[4]

These parables are not cute and cozy bedtime stories for our children to read. They are sarcastic, sucker-punching, pot-stirring, satire-laden tales that function like social grenades. Sometimes Jesus pulls the pin and the truth unavoidably explodes in the room. At other times he lights a time-delayed fuse, and only later do his listeners "get it." Sometimes those listeners, including we who read the stories today, do not "get it" at all.

A fisherman named Sam always seemed to catch fish when others could not. Some would bring in nothing but two or three small trout or nothing at all, and Sam would bring in a boat full. He was the envy of the local fishing trade. The game warden, more curious than suspicious, was interested in Sam's successful techniques. He asked if he could accompany Sam on his next venture. Sam was more than happy to oblige. On the appointed morning, Sam and the game warden met at the dock, climbed into Sam's boat, and headed out.

When they arrived at the right spot, far from shore and any other fishermen, Sam went to work. He reached into his tackle box and produced a stick of dynamite. He lit the fuse and chunked it overboard into the water. The air and water roared with the sound of the explosion. Shortly thereafter, fish began floating to the surface, killed and stunned by the percussion. Sam took his dip net and began collecting them off the top of the water. The game warden exploded with about the same ferocity as the stick of dynamite.

With his ears still ringing from the blast, he began screaming at Sam, "You can't do this! Who do you think you are? I'm going to write you a ticket for every offense in the book! I'm going to bury you *under* the jail! You will never finish paying the fine that will be levied against you, and you will never fish in this territory again!"

Sam looked at the officer for a moment or two. Then he reached into his tackle box, pulled out another stick of dynamite, lit it, and threw it into the lap of the game warden.

He asked him, "Are you gonna sit there all day complaining, or are you gonna fish?"[5]

Jesus' parables lie in our laps like lit sticks of dynamite, begging the question, "What are you going to do now?"

Will we hear the stories that Jesus tells as our own stories? Will we take the journey to Jerusalem with him as part of our own journey? Will we see that the people Jesus meets on his way to Jerusalem are not just Jewish peasants, thick-headed disciples, and fuming religionists? He is talking to you and me. We are pulled in not to analyze, but to participate. When we play our part in the story and when we join the journey, something happens that fixed propositions and doctrinal systems can never accomplish. Jesus begins to change our hearts and minds. He begins to undercut the foundations upon which we have built our beliefs and convictions. His stubborn drive to Jerusalem succeeds in melting our hearts of stone.

Doctrines, dogma, and encyclopedic principles for living: these are easy to ignore, easy to evade. But we cannot ignore being pulled into an inspired, living story in step with Jesus as he moves toward a destiny. Can we reject this path on which Jesus leads us? Yes. Can we escape or evade it? Impossible.

Along the meandering road to Jerusalem, Luke invites us to eavesdrop on stories we may have heard before, but to which we have not truly listened. On this journey, Luke lures us into tagging behind a Jesus who is the champion of sinners, outcasts, and the ethically questionable. Jesus brings to the table and restores to the family those excluded from the kingdom of God.

However, the religious establishment greets Jesus' mercy toward outsiders as blasphemy. It causes the good church folk to squirm in their seats. The well-mannered, honorable, rule-keeping Pharisees and experts of the law with their PhDs, spiritual paternity, and lectures in biblical interpretation are pitched against a dusty, barefoot carpenter from the hardscrabble town of Nazareth. He is rumored to be a bastard child, with nothing but a peasant's education and a penchant for heresy.

This gypsy named Jesus is a rebel, a "friend of sinners," and an irreligious radical. To dare to follow him is to heed his word of warning as the journey begins: "We are going to Jerusalem to die." Jesus and institutional religion are on a collision course, and those who go with Jesus will find more adventure, freedom, and religion-bursting grace than they can stand, all the things that make traveling worth the effort. But they will also find clash and conflict. The path of Jesus is not well tolerated by the establishment.

But if we do not take to this dusty road with Jesus to confront the religious conclusions of our own hearts, if we do not sit with the disciples at the storyteller's feet, immersing ourselves in these unconventional parables—parables so life-like that we can almost touch the suffering Lazarus, wipe the pig-pen grime from the neck of the prodigal son, and see the bag ladies and squeegee men stumbling off the street with toothless smiles into the banquet hall called the kingdom of God—then we risk staying put in our narrow, constricted, predictable ideas about religious obligation.

Not following Jesus is being unmoved, and being unmoved is risking the greatest danger of all: misunderstanding and misrepresenting God. For this journey, Jesus will use his stories, his interactions with the good-for-nothings and the questioners, and the confrontations he ignites with the religious leaders of his day to reveal things about God that destroy the status quo. He will reshape our conceptions of who God is and what God is doing in the world.

If we choose to follow this path, then all our previous understandings of God and religion, faith and spirituality, creed and Christ, might get torn down. Once these are ripped away, something better, larger, more gracious, and much more revolutionary than we ever imagined may replace them.

Ultimately, this is what this Great Journey of Jesus is all about. It is a revolution. Jesus is changing the state of affairs in the world and in our hearts. As he moves toward Jerusalem, the ground beneath our feet begins to shiver and shake, and we are invited to join the world-shattering revolution of following him.

We do not know where this journey will take us, but we cannot stay where we are. Jesus is on the move, and he calls us to join him.

Notes

1. William Shakespeare, *The Tragedy of Hamlet, Prince of Denmark* (New York: Washington Square Press, 1958), 64.

2. Joel B. Green, *The Theology of the Gospel of Luke* (New York: Cambridge University Press, 2006), 21.

3. Eugene H. Peterson, *The Message: The New Testament, Psalms and Proverbs* (Colorado Springs: Navpress, 1995), 146.

4. Michael Ball, *The Radical Stories of Jesus; Interpreting the Parables Today* (Oxford: Regent's, 2000), 72.

5. Adapted from Max Lucado, *No Wonder They Call Him the Savior* (Nashville: W Publishing, 2004), 121.

Reflection Questions

1. What journeys have you taken that have most affected your life? Why did these journeys influence you so greatly?

2. I use the term "holy propaganda" to describe Luke's arrangement of the Great Journey of Jesus. Is that an appropriate way to refer to a Gospel in our Bible? Why or why not?

3. How self-aware do you think Jesus was as he journeyed toward Jerusalem? How much did he know about what would happen to him?

4. The original band of twelve disciples had no clue where this journey with Jesus would take them. How much do we really understand when we begin following Christ?

5. Why do you think Jesus and institutional religion are on a "collision course"?

____

____

____

____

____

Chapter 2

The Greatest Story Ever Told

> If you judge people, you have no time to love them.
>
> —Mother Teresa

One of the more distressing stories of American urban life comes from the pages of the *New York Times* more than forty years ago.[1] It is a story that sociologists and their students have scrutinized and explored for decades. Still, it bears repeating.

A young lady named Catherine Genovese, a twenty-eight-year-old sports bar manager better known as Kitty, returned to her Queens apartment around 3:00 a.m. on the morning of March 13, 1964. She parked her car and began the short walk to her front door. Kitty noticed a suspicious man at the far end of the parking lot. His name was Winston Moseley. When Moseley started toward her, Kitty bolted and ran for home. He caught her, stabbing her twice in the back. She screamed out, "Oh, my God, he stabbed me! Please help me! Please help me!"

Lights came on in the apartment building across the street, windows opened, and a male voice called out, "Leave that girl alone!" Moseley slipped off into the darkness. Windows closed, lights went out, and everything was quiet again. Then the assailant returned and began stabbing Genovese again. Again she cried out, "My God! I'm dying! I'm dying!" Again windows opened, lights came on, voices called out into the dark. Winston Moseley once more scampered away into the night.

Kitty Genovese managed to crawl down the street to her apartment building. For a third time Moseley returned. He searched the parking lot and the small apartment complex until he found her. When he did, he sexually assaulted her, stole the $49 Kitty had in her purse, and finished the murder he had begun some thirty minutes earlier. Then, quite calmly, he returned to his car and drove away.

There were three separate attacks over the space of half an hour in three different locations. No one did a thing to intervene.

When Kitty's body was found, the police arrived in minutes. In the interviewing process, authorities discovered that dozens of people had witnessed or heard at least one of the attacks. Some were afraid to call. Others said they were too tired to understand what was happening. But the most common response was, "I did not want to get involved."

Tragically, according to the same publication, in an article dated December 27, 1974, ten years after Kitty's murder another young woman, Sandra Zahler, was beaten to death early Christmas morning in an apartment in the same building that overlooked the site of the Genovese attack. Again, neighbors said they heard screams and "fierce struggles" but did nothing to help.[2]

Would you stop to help a stranger who was being attacked? Would you help someone even if you knew that doing so could be costly, even to the point of risking your finances, your safety, or your life? Would you stop and help a friend who was in serious trouble? Would you intervene to save your spouse or one of your children?

It depends, I suppose, who is in trouble before we make the decision to get involved. The closer the person is to us, the more likely we are to lend a hand. The further they are from our inner circle, the more likely we are to do what one witness to the Genovese murder did—simply turn up the radio to drown out what is going on around the corner.

How far do we go in helping someone in need? Where should we limit our compassion? We cannot help everyone, can we? Where do we draw our ethical, moral, and neighborly lines? These are the questions asked of Jesus in Luke 10.

Who is my neighbor?

Who is in my community?

To whom do I owe the responsibility of help in a time of need?

Our first stop on Jesus' Great Journey to Jerusalem is a familiar one: the Parable of the Good Samaritan.

> One day an expert in religious law stood up to test Jesus by asking him this question: "Teacher, what should I do to inherit eternal life?"
>
> Jesus replied, "What does the law of Moses say? How do you read it?"
>
> The man answered, "'You must love the Lord your God with all your heart, all your soul, all your strength, and all your mind.' And, 'Love your neighbor as yourself.'"

"Right!" Jesus told him. "Do this and you will live!"

The man wanted to justify his actions, so he asked Jesus, "And who is my neighbor?"

Jesus replied with a story: "A Jewish man was traveling on a trip from Jerusalem to Jericho, and he was attacked by bandits. They stripped him of his clothes, beat him up, and left him half dead beside the road. By chance a priest came along. But when he saw the man lying there, he crossed to the other side of the road and passed him by. A temple assistant walked over and looked at him lying there, but he also passed by on the other side.

"Then a despised Samaritan came along, and when he saw the man, he felt compassion for him. Going over to him, the Samaritan soothed his wounds with olive oil and wine and bandaged them. Then he put the man on his own donkey and took him to an inn, where he took care of him. The next day he handed the innkeeper two silver coins, telling him, 'Take care of this man. If his bill runs higher than this, I'll pay you the next time I'm here.'

"Now which of these three would you say was a neighbor to the man who was attacked by bandits?" Jesus asked.

The man replied, "The one who showed him mercy."

Then Jesus said, "Yes, now go and do the same." (Luke 10:25-37)

A religious leader comes to Jesus with a question: "If loving God and loving my neighbor is the totality of religious and spiritual requirement, then tell me, Jesus, who is my neighbor?"

This parable is Jesus' answer, probably the greatest story he ever told. It is certainly his most well-known parable. The Good Samaritan turns up everywhere in our culture, even in places where people do not know what a Samaritan is or that Jesus first told the story. This story even framed the plot of the *Seinfeld* finale a few years ago.[3]

With such familiarity, we typically think of the Good Samaritan as a parable about being a good neighbor. That is not Jesus' point at all. Jesus does not even attempt to define the word "neighbor," though that is what the religious questioner wanted. Jesus takes another tack altogether. He defines instead what it means to "love your neighbor." It is a love that involves itself in unexpected, revolutionary, boundary-breaking ways.

The story begins with an unfortunate traveler on the Jericho Road. Jesus' original listeners were more than familiar with the dangers of traveling between Jerusalem and Jericho. The road connecting the two cities, if we begin in Jerusalem as Jesus does with the story, winds and turns for seventeen miles, dropping into the Rift Valley some three thousand feet below. It is a steep, downhill journey. That is dangerous enough, but it is not the real danger on this road. The Jericho Road was infamously unsafe because of thieves and robbers—roving bands of hooligans who preyed on caravans, merchants, and individual travelers.

The church father Jerome still referred to this road as "The Bloody Way" some five hundred years after the story was told.[4] Even a millennium after its telling, the Jericho Road was still a dangerous place to travel. It was so dangerous that the Templers, who have attracted a great deal of contemporary attention, were stationed along the road to protect crusading pilgrims from bandits in the twelfth century.[5]

If Jesus told this story in a different time, he would have matched the context of his hearers. If he told it, say, in the American West of the 1800s, he might make the traveler a Pony Express rider, ambushed by the Apache or a band of outlaws. If he were telling this story in modern-day Iraq, he might describe a U.S. diplomat caught outside the Green Zone without an escort and attacked by local militia. If he were telling this story in Rio de Janeiro today, he might describe a European tourist abducted for ransom by a radical death squad in advance of the carnival celebrations.

This much is clear: the road to Jericho was a bad place to travel alone, and sure enough, our traveler is mugged, beaten, and left for dead. As dramatic as this is, in Jesus' telling of the story, the beating is only the prelude to the real drama.

There are two other travelers on the road in Jesus' story. They come upon the victim in quick succession. The first is a priest. The second is a temple assistant, or as some translations call him, a Levite. Again, the contextualization is perfect. The priest and temple assistant represent the religious professionals of Jesus' day. Think of the priest as a church pastor or a member of the clergy. The temple assistant is an associate minister, the minister of music, or perhaps a church administrator.

These are, to use our own Christian language, "good church people." Remember, the question of a religious professional, a good church person, sparked this parable in the first place. Slyly, Jesus puts the religious professionals and representatives of the establishment into his story as main characters. What do these characters do? Nothing. They refuse to intervene.

Actually, "nothing" is too strong of a word. Both the priest and temple assistant do something. They see the beaten victim lying along the side of the road, and they "pass by on the other side." They intentionally move over. Like catching the stench of something wretched, they put distance between themselves and their neighbor in need, treating him as little more than roadkill.

Why did they do this? Well, they were obeying "the law." Leviticus 21 and Numbers 19 instruct temple workers not to contaminate themselves by touching a dead body. By law, if they touched a dead body that did not belong to their immediate family, they were declared ceremonially and religiously "unclean" for seven days. This meant they could not go to the temple to worship, could not make sacrifices, could not burn incense or lead the songs of worship—to the penalty box they went. They would sit there for seven days, and only when the religious timeout ended were they allowed to return to service.

Priests and temple workers served on a rotation basis at the temple, sometimes working only two weeks a year. If these two religious professionals helped this guy, reached out and touched him and found him dead, or had him die in their arms, they risked being disqualified from half their temple service for a year. That was too big a risk to take. These good church people did what good church people do—they kept the rules and protected their purity. In the process, they ignored justice and mercy toward someone in need.

In a stroke of masterful Lucan irony, note where the priest and temple assistant are going: they are going *down* the road. That is, they are going from Jerusalem down into the Rift Valley to Jericho. It is no coincidence that Jesus portrays the religious establishment and its leaders moving *away* from Jerusalem, the City of God, while he has just embarked on this journey *to* Jerusalem. They are going in opposite directions. The two, Jesus on one hand and the rule-keeping religionists on the other, are out of sync, out of step, and on a collision course.

This is the point of the journey. Jesus' message is God's kingdom message of grace, mercy, and restoration. Jesus and the kingdom of God he brings are moving in one direction, and religion is moving in another. The result is seismic conflict as these two crash against one another. This becomes devastatingly clear to Jesus' listeners with the arrival of the story's hero: the Good Samaritan.

There is a tale about a man who went to his doctor with bandages on both of his ears. The doctor, of course, asked him what happened. The man said, "The telephone rang and I answered the iron instead." The doctor asked what happened to the other ear. The man said, "They called back."

A twist in this story is expected, but this twist, where a Samaritan is made into such a champion of compassion that he makes Israel's religious leaders look like calloused cynics, is out-and-out scandalous.[6] It burns the ears. It would be nothing less than the pastor serving real wine in the little plastic communion cups at my mother and father's conservative little mountain church. It would be like one of my children shouting out a forbidden curse word in the middle of the supermarket (which has happened, embarrassingly enough). When the Samaritan takes his place on center stage, all the air gets sucked out of the room. Sweat beads pop out above quivering lips. Seat cushions tighten against backsides.

"What? What did he just say? A Samaritan?"

Jesus pulls the pin on a social grenade and lobs it into the laps of his listeners.

To the Jews, Samaritans were societal and racial half-breeds. Some five hundred years before Christ, Jews from the northern region of Palestine intermarried with the Assyrians. In turn, they left behind their cultural identity and contaminated their ethnic purity. They even developed a competing religion, abandoning the Jewish temple for a house of worship on Mount Gerizim.

Do not miss the Lucan irony once again: a racial, cultural, and religious inferior is pitted against racial, cultural, and religious perfection. The inferior—the villain, the hated nemesis, the butt of racial jokes and ethnic slurs—turns out to be the hero.

Jesus might as well have shown up at an IRA meeting in Northern Ireland and made a good English Protestant the hero of the story. This would be like Jesus crashing a rally of the Ku Klux Klan and going on and on about the nobility and goodness of Martin Luther King, Jr. It would be the equivalent of telling this story at the Pentagon, making the priest a general, the temple assistant a Special Forces operative, and the Samaritan a Pakistani man with ties to Al Qaeda. The contrast is that bold and dangerous. It sounds harmless to us, but in its context, it is a bombshell.

Or maybe Jesus would tell it like this: A man was going down from Bainbridge, Georgia, to Tallahassee, Florida. Along the way the traveler had a flat tire. Stranded on the side of the road, he was robbed, his car was stripped, and he was shot and left for dead. A Baptist pastor, on his way home from the Southern Baptist Convention, saw the man, but he had a report to deliver to his congregation about the virtuous resolutions passed at the meeting he had attended and an important sermon to preach about our culture's deteriorating family values. Besides that, his children were in the car with him, and he refused to traumatize them with this carnage. So he never took his foot off the accelerator.

A few minutes later, a bishop of the Methodist church drove by. A successful woman, she sat on the board of Focus on the Family, the National Association of Evangelicals, and Concerned Women for America. Considering the scene before her, she concluded that her work in these organizations must continue. It was the only way to stop such meaningless acts of violence; violence most likely perpetrated by dangerous gangs of teenagers who were the products of broken homes and without the proper Judeo-Christian guidance. She was a mile past the scene of the crime before she called 911.

Then a third traveler came upon the victim: A gay man. A man with booze on his breath and marijuana in his bloodstream. A man who had not darkened the door of a church since he went with his Catholic grandmother to mass when he was a child. He saw the shooting victim and his heart was broken with compassion. He steered his car to the side of the road and jumped out with a first aid kit and a bottle of water. He bandaged the wounded man best he could, loaded him into the back seat of his car, and drove as quickly as possible back to Tallahassee Memorial Hospital.

There, this good neighbor checked his rescued friend into the emergency room. He gave the receptionist a copy of his own driver's license. He arranged for the transport of what was left of the victim's car. He then went to the hospital administrator and left a blank check, saying, "I don't know if this man has health insurance or not, but I will stand good for the bill regardless."

Now I ask you the question of Jesus: "Which of these three do you think was a neighbor to the man who fell into the hands of robbers?"

Wait a minute! You can't twist Jesus' story like this! You can't make someone like *that* out to be a Good Samaritan. You can't make a homosexual the hero and turn men and women of God into criminals by retelling this parable!

No? When he first told this story, Jesus tendered a possibility so radical it was inconceivable by the religious community; it was so scandalously radical, it was nothing less than a heresy.

Oddball. Outcast. Redneck. White trash. Squatter. Albino. Gook. Gangster. Wetback. Towel-head. Whatever name we have for whatever group we want to exclude, the Jews had a single description: Samaritan. Yet Jesus, a

Jew, took this pariah and made him the hero of one of the greatest stories ever told. We have read this story so many times that our familiarity with it deafens us to how shattering it truly is.

See, this is not a story about defining the boundaries of our neighborhood. This is a story about what it means to love. It is a story about what it means to be like God. To be like God is to be bold enough to break religious rules for the sake of kindness and mercy. This is a story about how those who do not fit into our religious boxes, doctrinal outlines, and church systems are more capable of acting like God than we professionals who pride ourselves on saying we know who God is.

Let me remind you: The priest and temple assistant were playing by the rules. They were not allowed to touch someone dead or dying. Such an act would contaminate them. They passed by on the other side of the road for the sake of moral purity, for the sake of holiness, and for the sake of all that was right. In the process they got it all wrong. This Samaritan was in the place of real holiness because he cared for someone in need. To be like God is not to have perfect doctrinal integrity, to get the details of church "right," or to be religiously and moralistically pure. To be like God is to dirty our hands with the labor of love.

Clucking our tongues, shedding a few tears, peering across the road at our neighbors who are in the ditch while protecting our religious credibility and respectability is no substitute for binding wounds, wiping tears, and understanding that all dead and dying people we encounter *are* in our immediate family, and we must reach out and embrace them. The command to love our neighbor is not just for our neighbor. It is for us as well. For when we love, we are brought into alignment with who God is as revealed by Jesus Christ.

Paul Rusesabagina is the former hotel manager who inspired the movie *Hotel Rwanda.* Beginning in April 1994, over the course of a hundred days, an estimated one million Rwandans were killed after extremists in the majority Hutu population turned on the Tutsi minority. Fifteen percent of the population was annihilated. For perspective, that would be the percentage equivalent of a genocide wiping out forty-six million Americans, the total combined population of the greater southeastern United States: Alabama, Georgia, Florida, Mississippi, South Carolina, and Tennessee—every human being living in those states gone in three months.

Hotel Rwanda focuses on the seventy-six days in which Paul Rusesabagina transformed the luxury hotel over which he was responsible into a refuge for the terrified.

In his memoir, *An Ordinary Man*, Paul talks about what happened when literally overnight, his friends and neighbors were brutally murdered and other friends and neighbors became frenzied, cold-blooded murderers. On the first day of violence, twenty-six people came to Paul's home for shelter. They knew he was a person of influence with high connections and that he could help them. That is why they came. But they also knew he was a person of compassion. He had grown up in the Seventh Day Adventist Church and studied theology before becoming a hotel manager. His father had also taught him always to do what is right, no matter the consequences.

His father would say to him, "If two brothers [are] fighting, and you are called upon to separate [them], you shouldn't look at those guys, one on your right hand side, or [on] the left hand side. . . . You only have to look up and see the truth, and only the truth." That truth became a shining light of compassion when, at the end of those three months of killings, Paul Rusesabagina had sheltered and saved 1,268 people in his hotel.[7] They all survived through the ingenuity and creativity of an ordinary hospitality worker who somehow kept corn and beans in the kitchen, rationed the water in the pool for drinking when militia cut the pipes, and removed the room numbers from the doors and burned the registration records so the roving bands of machete-welding killers would not know the identities of those under his protection. Not a single person in his hotel was killed; not a hair off one head was harmed.

At one point, Paul and his family were given the opportunity to leave Rwanda. He packed his bags to depart. It was then that the residents of his hotel came to him and said, "Paul, we know you are going to be leaving this place tomorrow. But please, if you are really leaving, tell us, because we will go to the roof of the hotel and jump. A better death would be to jump and die immediately than to be tortured."

Paul later said, "By that afternoon I had made the toughest decision of my life. I said to myself, 'Listen, Paul, if you leave, and those people are killed, you will never be a free man. You will be a prisoner of your own conscience.' I then decided to remain behind."[8]

He further explained his actions this way: "If I am going to die, then I will die helping my neighbor."[9]

A few years ago I preached from the Parable of the Good Samaritan as a visiting minister, filling the Sunday vacancy of a friend. I was running late and got to the church just before the morning worship service began. I walked in, went to the pulpit, and immediately gave the talk with no time for the customary glad-handing, introductions, and "hellos." A few people in attendance looked at me a little strange during the talk.

After the service, the associate minister came to me with a smile and she said, "You did that, didn't you?"

I just looked at her.

"Did what?" I asked.

"Oh, come on! I know you did it. Who was it?"

I was confused. I had no idea what she was talking about.

She then explained that between Sunday school and the worship service, just before I arrived, the elders of the church had conferred with a street man. He was a beggar needing help. The elders turned him away without a dime, without a single night's stay in a hotel, without so much as a meal or a referral to the Salvation Army or a shelter. With so much abuse by those who ask for help, the elders made their decision in the name of being "good stewards" of the money given to the church. But after my Good Samaritan discourse, they all left thinking the entire episode was just a test exercise of sorts, set up by the visiting preacher to strengthen his sermon. They wiped the sweat from their brows and continued with business as usual.

I can almost guarantee you that this story of the Good Samaritan and all its implications will come to bear on your life before these words grow cold in your mind. You will come across one who needs a hand, who needs compassion, who needs the mercy of God, who needs the love of a friend. You might even get put in the uncomfortable position of having to choose between keeping the religious rules or actually doing what is right.

May you choose the latter, because if this story teaches us anything it is this: business as usual is no longer usual.

Notes

1. Martin Gansberg, "37 Who Say Murder Didn't Call Police," *New York Times*, 27 March 1964, 1.

2. Robert D. McFadden, "A Model's Dying Screams Are Ignored at the Site of Kitty Genovese's Murder," *New York Times*, 27 December 1974, 65.

3. "A Tough Nut to Crack," *Seinfeld*, episode 180, written by Larry David and Jerry Seinfeld, directed by Andy Ackerman, NBC, 14 May 1998.

4. William Barclay, *The Parables of Jesus* (Louisville: Westminster John Knox, 1999), 79.

5. David Wenham, *The Parables of Jesus* (Downers Grove IL: Intervarsity Press, 1989), 155.

6. Leon Morris, *Tyndale New Testament Commentaries, Revised: Luke* (Grand Rapids: Eerdmans, 1995), 207.

7. Paul Rusesabagina, *An Ordinary Man: An Autobiography* (New York: Viking, 2006) passim.

8. Courtney Waters, "Rusesabagina Urges Greater Awareness," 30 January 2008, http://newsnet.byu.edu/story.cfm/67198 (accessed 5 February 2008); Michelle Ye Hee Lee, "An Interview with Paul Rusesabagina," 19 October 2007, http://www.emory-wheel.com/detail.php?n=24481 (accessed 5 February 2008).

9. Brian McLaren, "God in the Movies: *Hotel Rwanda*," 16 October 2005, sermon.

Reflection Questions

1. Recall a time when you had the opportunity to help someone in need. Why did you help them? Why not?

2. Is there a difference between the rules dictated by the establishment and what is actually right? Explain.

3. I bring the Good Samaritan story forward by retelling it in a modern setting. Is this an accurate interpretation, or does it push Jesus' story too far? Why or why not?

4. "To be like God is to dirty our hands with the labor of love." Explain whether you agree or disagree with this statement.

5. Place yourself in Paul Rusesabagina's shoes. Can you begin to feel his fear and tension as he helped his neighbors? What gave him the courage to act so definitively?

___

___

___

___

___

Chapter 3

Wear Your Religion Like You Wear Your Underwear

Watch out for all who do not walk in simplicity.
—The Schleitheim Confession

I heard about a man who lacked the art of diplomacy. He was the type of person who couldn't say anything graciously.

He and his wife owned a poodle. They loved the dog. It was like a child to them. The wife took a trip away from home, and on the first day away she called to see how things were going.

She asked her husband, "How are things?"

He answered, "The dog is dead!"

She was devastated. After regaining her composure, she asked, "Why did you do that? Why can't you be more thoughtful, more tactful?"

He said, "Well, what do you want me to say? The dog is dead."

She said, "Well, you could have given it to me in stages. For example, you could have said, 'The dog is on the roof.' Then when I called you the next day, you could say, 'Everything is fine here, except the dog fell off the roof.' When I called you the third day you could have added, 'Oh, the dog had to be taken to the vet. He's not doing very well.' Finally, when I called you on the last day of my trip, you could have said, 'Honey, brace yourself, our beloved dog has died.' I could have handled it better than you being so severe."

Her husband paused. She could tell he was taking it all in.

Finally he said, "OK, I see."

Then she asked, "By the way, how is mother?"

He answered, "Well, your mother is on the roof."[1]

In the first church I pastored, I knew an old man who'd been a master sergeant longer than I had been alive, and he had spent most of those years drunk. He drank a pint of bourbon before lunch every day and then tried to cut his grass on one of those old Snapper lawnmowers, with his knees pointed out like door knobs, weaving all over the place. He got sober sometime around his sixtieth birthday, gave his life to Christ, and became a deacon in the Baptist church.

He was a changed man, but a part of him that did not change was his punchy, master sergeant mentality (that and the two packs of Camels he smoked every day). He griped and complained and barked orders at everyone like we were all new, green recruits. He and I fought like an old married couple, and there were times when I thought we would never agree on anything. Still, I never doubted that he loved me. We would duke it out in a church meeting one evening and meet for coffee at the local greasy spoon the next morning. I think he enjoyed mixing it up with others.

He and I argued one day because he wanted to confront someone harshly. I suggested a kinder, gentler, and patient approach.

He growled at me, "That's your problem, preacher! You want to beat around the bush with people when something needs to be said."

I fired back, "I might beat around the bush, but at least the tree will live when I am finished. You're pulling it up by the roots!"

God rest his good soul, and those of master sergeants everywhere, but that man loved Luke 11:37-53. There, Jesus takes a verbal whipping stick to the religious leaders of his day.

In the story of the Good Samaritan (Luke 10:30-37), Jesus is subtle and sarcastic as he draws the teachers of the law into his web. He playfully but clearly identifies them as the "bad guys." "The dog is on the roof," Jesus began as he told that particular parable. But not in Luke 11. Rather than shaking the outer branches of the tree, he grabs it by the trunk and pulls it up at the roots.

If Jesus did not have our attention in Luke 10, he certainly has it by the end of Luke 11:

> As Jesus was speaking, one of the Pharisees invited him home for a meal. So he went in and took his place at the table. His host was amazed to see that he sat down to eat without first performing the hand-washing ceremony required by Jewish custom. Then the Lord said to him, "You Pharisees are so careful to clean the outside of the cup and the dish, but

> inside you are filthy—full of greed and wickedness! Fools! Didn't God make the inside as well as the outside? So clean the inside by giving gifts to the poor, and you will be clean all over.
>
> "What sorrow awaits you Pharisees! For you are careful to tithe even the tiniest income from your herb gardens, but you ignore justice and the love of God. You should tithe, yes, but do not neglect the more important things. What sorrow awaits you Pharisees! For you love to sit in the seats of honor in the synagogues and receive respectful greetings as you walk in the marketplaces. Yes, what sorrow awaits you! For you are like hidden graves in a field. People walk over them without knowing the corruption they are stepping on."
>
> "Teacher," said an expert in religious law, "you have insulted us, too, in what you just said."
>
> "Yes," said Jesus, "what sorrow also awaits you experts in religious law! For you crush people with unbearable religious demands, and you never lift a finger to ease the burden. What sorrow awaits you! For you build monuments for the prophets your own ancestors killed long ago. But in fact, you stand as witnesses who agree with what your ancestors did. They killed the prophets, and you join in their crime by building the monuments! This is what God in his wisdom said about you: 'I will send prophets and apostles to them, but they will kill some and persecute the others.' As a result, this generation will be held responsible for the murder of all God's prophets from the creation of the world—from the murder of Abel to the murder of Zechariah, who was killed between the altar and the sanctuary. Yes, it will certainly be charged against this generation.
>
> "What sorrow awaits you experts in religious law! For you remove the key to knowledge from the people. You don't enter the kingdom yourselves, and you prevent others from entering."
>
> As Jesus was leaving, the teachers of religious law and the Pharisees became hostile and tried to provoke him with many questions. They wanted to trap him into saying something they could use against him. (Luke 11:37-53)

Some two hundred years before the time of Christ, the Jewish people united in a war of independence called the Maccabean War. They fought against Antiochus Epiphanies, the king of Syria. They were successful in gaining independence, but the aftermath resulted in a religious and political vacuum. The Jewish society had to learn to live in the brave new world they created. One of the groups that developed during this period became known as the Pharisees. In Luke 11, Jesus exchanges blistering words with this group at a dinner party in the home of one of the more prominent Pharisees.

The Pharisees were the "pious ones" or the "puritans," not unlike the Puritans of our own American history. Their passion was the Jewish religion. They were deeply devoted to the written Law of Moses, the Torah, and their oral traditions, later called the Mishnah or the Talmud. It was the Pharisaic duty to obey the written and unwritten laws of God, to remain ceremonially pure, and to live righteously enough to enjoy the resurrection from the dead one day.

By the time of Jesus, the Pharisees were the largest and most influential religious party in Palestine. They ran the schools and the academies. The priests and scribes were members of their order. In time, they developed an eschatology or end-of-the-world scenario about the coming of the messiah and the end of the age. They believed the messiah would not come until people adopted and lived out proper religious practice down to the tiniest details of life. When Jewish society, through the Pharisees' untiring efforts, became righteous and holy enough, then the kingdom of God would break into the world.

For the sake of clarity, we might benefit from seeing these Pharisees of Jesus' day as fervent fundamentalists who were theological watchdogs. They knew what the Bible said. They knew what God expected. They had orthodoxy and tradition on their side.

Their conclusion was that life would be much better and their society and nation more successful if only everyone else got with the program—*their* program. If everyone else believed like they believed, acted like they acted, and behaved like they behaved, then God would show his blessing on Israel, throw off the foreign oppressors, send the messiah, and consign the remaining sinners to hell. I do not have to overstate the obvious: these Pharisees seem terribly familiar.

In Luke 11, Jesus attends a dinner party with a handful of Pharisees. While there, he makes a serious social and religious faux pas at the table. Jesus fails to wash his hands before he eats. This would have gotten me turned away from my grandmother's dining room table as well, but for different reasons. My grandmother wanted my hands clean from germs. The Pharisees however, had an extensive hand-washing system that was religious, not necessarily hygienic in nature.

The Pharisees washed their hands with their fingers pointed upward, the water running down and dripping from their wrists and elbows. Wringing the hands free of water was not allowed. This would mingle clean water with the dirty water, and the bather would still be considered unclean. So the Pharisees would stand there until their hands had dripped dry, and then they would repeat the process with fingers pointed to the ground so the unclean water would again run off properly.

Strict Jews did this before every meal. If they were especially devout, as these dinner guests with Jesus probably were, they repeated the process even between the courses of the meal. It could take hours to finish eating. Jesus probably ignored the hand-washing bowl put before him on purpose in order to stoke the crowd. As soon as his dinner companions saw his behavior, before they even finished their hurried whispers and stopped rolling their eyes, he spoke thunderous words down on their heads.

I know a little about public speaking. I know that when speaking to a group of people, it is best to know their background, their preferences, their likes and dislikes. This is important in order for the speaker to build rapport and gain the audience's respect. I guess Jesus didn't take that course in seminary, because here he lets loose with a verbal tirade. Additionally, he offends his host—the one who invited him to dinner in the first place. Offense or not, Jesus tells the truth, in all of its bold, tactless ugliness.

This truth comes down in a series of "what sorrows" or, as other English translations put it, "woes." At first, these seem like statements of condemnation. Yet, it is more accurate to view them as statements of grief, not judgment. Jesus' words in this encounter have a pessimistic nature. "You are a pitiful bunch," Jesus is saying. "As pathetic as you are, there is not much anyone can do about it."

I don't want to say Jesus viewed these religious leaders as hopeless, but I also don't want to lessen his criticism of them. He pronounces the first three statements of sorrow specifically on the Pharisees.[2] These accusations focus on three odd points: (1) the spices in their cupboards; (2) where they sit in church; and (3) graveyards.

First, they tithed *everything*, even their spices. The Pharisees were so meticulous about keeping every single commandment of written law and oral tradition that they did more than just tithe out of their money. They tithed all the way down to the salt in their shakers. Every Sabbath, they went to their spice racks. They measured out ten percent, down to counting individual grains, and then took it to the synagogue or the temple and presented it as an offering.

While they spent all their time focused on minutiae, the Pharisees neglected justice and love. They violated the great commandment to love God and love their neighbors by trivializing love and compassion in favor of keeping rules.

Second, the Pharisees were concerned with seats in the synagogue and greetings in the streets. With tongue in cheek, Jesus said these Pharisees loved for others to see them practicing their religion. They loved to sit up front during the worship service—on the platform, on a stage, elevated and exalted, appreciated and praised for being such holy persons who had done so much for God.

Out on the street corner was no different. Some Pharisees planned their trip to the market just before prayer time, so that when the bells tolled for prayer, they stopped wherever they were, right in the middle of the street if necessary, and began saying long, loud prayers so that everything around them came to a screeching halt.

"Look at him," the passersby said. "Look how holy he is."

Jesus viewed such showmen as arrogant fools.

"Go say your prayers in a closet, not in front of the crowds," Jesus was saying. "Be content to sit in the back of the synagogue and not on the stage. Hide from your left hand what your right hand is putting in the offering plate. Quit bragging about how often you go to church. God doesn't care about the size of that red Bible tucked beneath your arm. He is not impressed by your fifty-eight years' worth of perfect Sunday school attendance pins—not when you are more interested in your own perfection than the poor and needy."

Jesus would agree with Landon Saunders, who says, "We should wear our religion like we wear our underwear. Make it rarely visible."[3]

Third, Jesus called these Pharisees a field of unmarked graves. Recall that in the story of the Good Samaritan, the priest and temple assistant refused to aid the man who suffered at the hands of thieves. They did not want to risk religious contamination. Touching a dying man, a dead man, would disqualify them from religious service and worship in the temple. To touch the dying was to break the law. Without a doubt, some who heard Jesus tell the story then sat around the table with Jesus in the incident of Luke 11, and he turned the tables on them.

He essentially said, "You won't touch the dying—you won't show mercy and compassion—for the sake of keeping the rules. But every person who crosses your path, every person you encounter, you are poisoning and contaminating them with the death that you call faithfulness. You are concerned about staying clean, but you are already dead, and killing others in the process."

The sin that Jesus so plainly condemned was the pride and arrogance inherent with religion. "You condemn my dirty hands? You have dirty hearts." "You brag about how much you give to the church? You have not given yourself to alleviate the suffering of your neighbors." "You want to be seen and heard at worship and when you pray? God quit listening to you a long time ago."

Religious pride—the smug sense of being right at the expense of others—is a terrifying cause of suffering in this world that other sources of misery rarely match. Arrogance, driven by religion, is poisonous spirituality.

On September 13, 1987, two young men scavenged a partially demolished medical clinic in Goianaia, Brazil. The two men were unemployed and hoped to find something they could use to make a few bucks. They found a bulky machine that they intended to reduce to parts and sell. Inside the machine was a stainless steel cylinder, about the size of a gallon paint can. They sold the cylinder to a junk dealer for $25.

Inside the cylinder was a crumbly powder that glowed a mysterious blue. The junk dealer took the "magic material" home and shared it with his friends and family. His six-year-old niece rubbed it on like body paint. She sang and danced, radiant with the blue dust.

The blue dust was not magic. It was cesium-137, one of the most dangerous radioactive isotopes in the world. The stolen machine was once used to give cancer patients their radiation treatments. The little girl and several others died within hours. Hundreds more were sickened and contaminated.[4] Here was this beautiful, radiant dust, broken out of a machine intended to heal the body, that now became an instrument of death. The story is a powerful metaphor for religion.

Religion. Faithfulness. Commitment. Orthodoxy. Purity. Conviction. These all begin with material taken from a holy book, church doctrine, or some kernel of truth; from a well that is intended to bring spiritual healing and wholeness. In the end, these can become a poison that rots the bones. Certainly, the Pharisees did not begin with the intention of poisoning their society with religion. Likewise, we never intend to go down the path of arrogance and soul-damning pride. It is always a journey that begins with good intentions, but as the proverb tells us, we know where good intentions can lead.

If we embrace Jesus as less than the insurrectionist he was, then we are sliding down the slope into the religious graveyard. Jesus did not come to start a religion. He came to blow religion off the map. Jesus did not come to tinker with our ideas about God. He came to show us who God really is. Jesus did not come to build cathedrals or pulpits. He came to start a revolution. Jesus came to initiate a way of life, a new way to live, that knocks the props from beneath everything else we have ever known.

In Luke 11, Jesus is not yet finished at the dinner table. He keeps his dining companions between the hammer and the anvil for a while longer. An expert in the religious law speaks up to defend the Pharisees, who up to this point have received the sharp end of Jesus' words.

These experts in the law were like teachers, seminary professors, and others with post-graduate studies in ancient Hebrew. Often they were the copyists and trusted interpreters of the biblical text. They transcribed the ancient texts and oral traditions on paper. Those who did this kind of work, as you might imagine, became the leading authorities on the text. They had authority because they had knowledge, and they sought to preserve Judaism against all heretical opponents, including someone like Jesus. So while the Pharisees were the practitioners of the law, these experts, teachers, and "scribes" as they were sometimes called, were the research scientists, the specialists working behind the scenes.

In the Scripture, one of these professors speaks up to defend his friends, the Pharisees. Imagine that Jesus sits at the head of a long, rectangular table—the place of honor since everyone wants to speak with him. Thus far he has spoken to the Pharisees, seated to his left. As Jesus takes them to task, to his right one of the experts in the religious law interjects, "Excuse me, rabbi. When you say such things, we find it to be terribly offensive."

Granted, he makes a valiant attempt to protect his friends, but his words only draw fire. Smack, smack, smack: Jesus now turns to the other side of the table and the punches resume. The Pharisees get the first three. The experts and teachers of the law get the last three.

Here, as before, Jesus levels three indictments: (1) your religion crushes the people you teach; (2) you resort to violence and exploitation against anyone who disagrees with you; and (3) you have locked the door to people's minds while keeping your own mind locked shut, throwing away the key.

If the Pharisees are condemned for their pride and arrogance, then these experts in the law are condemned for the crime of coercion and manipulation, of unmercifully intimidating and fear-mongering people into religious submission. Put the pride of the Pharisees and the bullying of the religious experts together, and you confront the most threatening two-headed monster possible. It is religious oppression at its worst. If you want to make Jesus angry, let this monster raise its ugly head. Jesus will push against it with a vengeance.

Here is how the teachers of the law operated: the Torah, or the Old Testament Law, consisting of the first five books of the Bible, contains 613 individual commandments; 365 of these are negative: "Thou shalt not." Of the 613 commandments, 248 are positive: "Thou shalt."

That is heavy enough. Most of us are not aware that there are so many different ways to disobey. Add to that the commandments of the oral tradition—the law experts' specialty. The oral tradition, which later became the Talmud, translates into English as a thirty-six-volume set of more than 7,000 pages. To put it in perspective, the latest *Webster's Collegiate Dictionary* has *only* about 1,500 pages.[5]

The law experts laid this massive quantity of material upon the backs of a largely illiterate society. The throng of Jewish farmers, shepherds, and peasants could not read or write, at least not competently. If they had any spiritual inclination, they depended on the religious establishment to guide them toward God. The members of this establishment, recognizing their monopoly on all things divine, held the people hostage. They kept the people in the pew under their thumb. They eliminated any and all dissent. They locked away the simple understanding of loving God and loving neighbors, and they built roadblock after roadblock in the way of people just trying to get to God.

Ancient Greek mythology includes the story of a fellow named Sisyphus. I know: his name sounds like a communicable disease. But in Greek mythology, Sisyphus was a great king and founder of the city of Corinth. In his day he was an entrepreneurial genius, but his tactics left a little to be desired. He operated more like the Godfather than Jack Welch.

Sisyphus was a deceptive, murderous, untrustworthy scoundrel. If you read the mythologies about him, you find that Sisyphus so irritated the gods that they banished him to Hades on at least two or three occasions, depending upon which writer you read. Still, Sisyphus was such a wily character that he could even negotiate escapes from the underworld.

Finally, the gods caught up with him and condemned him to an eternity of frustrating back-breaking labor, rolling a huge boulder to the top of a hill. It took all his strength to complete the task, and every time Sisyphus arrived at the top with his rock, the stone rolled back down to the bottom. Sisyphus was forced to begin the process all over again.

The experts in the religious law played the role of the Greek gods in Jewish society. As soon as the people got their rock of religious obligation and rule-keeping to the top of the mountain, the religious specialists kicked it back into the valley with another assignment, a new requirement, a more accurate interpretation of Scripture.

"You have to do better."

"You have to try harder."

"You need to give more."

"You must pray longer."

"You need to attend more often."

"You are not good enough."

Spirituality became a dreadfully heavy burden to push up the hill. It became an exhausting deathtrap.

For those of us who have lived most of our lives under the shadow of a steeple, these may be hard words to take. When Jesus assaults institutional religion, he assaults our familiar way of belief. Even so, I must admit my own bias here. I like Jesus' attacks.

I get angry when I see Pharisaic pride and coercion at work in the name of God. This is a sensitive spot for me, for I was raised in a legalistic religious system that would have made the Pharisees proud. For as far back as I can remember, I was put to work pushing the rock up the hill.

I could tell you stories about how women in the churches of my childhood were publicly humiliated because people saw them out in the community wearing a pair of earrings or too much makeup or too short a skirt. I could rage about how the pastor and board of deacons confronted my own father because his job prevented him from getting to church on Wednesday nights. He was told he should quit that job "in order to please God," and that not doing so was showing "a lack of trust in God" to take care of his family. I could recount how people who posited interpretations of Scripture that differed from those of the church leadership were openly rebuked and disciplined. They were quickly told that it was a great sin to question those God had placed in authority.

My childhood church was such a constricted environment that I left as a teenager. I joined a Southern Baptist Church. That's right, I was raised in such a legalistic setting that I *wanted* to be a Southern Baptist. This new church had a youth group that actually enjoyed being together and attending church. The pastor read from a version of the Bible that was refreshingly post-Shakespearean. Women were allowed to speak from the pulpit. This new church of mine even cancelled Sunday night services on occasion. Remarkable!

When I left the legalistic system of my childhood, the leaders of that church refused to grant my membership to the "less-than-orthodox" congregation on the other side of town. Later, when I was ordained to the ministry as a young adult, people who had known me my entire life refused to attend the service because the path I had chosen seemed too far outside their comfortable corner of fundamentalism. Additionally, I had abandoned the authorized King James Version of the Bible. Clearly, this is a sensitive subject for me.

It is a sensitive subject for another reason as well. After my ordination, I jumped into church work with both feet. I set the religious world on fire, and at the childish age of twenty-four I became pastor of a little storefront church. We bought a huge tract of land. We built hundreds of thousands of dollars worth of buildings. We quadrupled in size. We added pastoral staff. We gave tons of money to missions and other service organizations. Not yet thirty years old, I was involved in the executive leadership of my state denomination, assisting in the allocation of millions of ecclesiological dollars, rubbing shoulders with the religious superstars, and on the way to becoming one myself.

Then, while shaving at the sink early one morning, with my personal and spiritual life in the toilet, I looked at myself in the mirror. Tears made trails through the white cream. I replayed in my mind the things I was saying. I took an inventory of where I was and where I was going, and I felt ashamed. I had become the thing I once despised, the thing I promised myself I would always avoid. I was a hard-core, unyielding legalist with more pride and manipulation than the worst Pharisee.

I embraced and "loved" people only if they kept the rules, even though I charmingly smiled when talking about those rules. I spent time with people, incalculable amounts of time, if I was sure they would become a member of my congregation. I became excruciatingly sensitive to those who wrote the biggest checks, and ensured they were "serving the church" in the most opportune places. I applauded those who agreed with me and my ministerial visions, and quietly but firmly marginalized those who did not.

I worked hard to live up to the unyielding expectations of my religious system and the people around me, while deftly manipulating that same system and those same people to meet my own expectations and get what I wanted. May God forgive me for this. I live, like many, I think, with this two-edged sensitivity of having suffered abuse by lethal religion and, as with any cycle of exploitation, becoming the abuser myself.

I may sound like an Old Testament prophet when I say this, but may God deal with me, be it ever so severely, if I do not offer the one thing Jesus offered to the world in the face of religious poison: mercy. That is what we all need. Even—especially—we religionists.

This struggle, Jesus' struggle, is not against flesh and blood. Our quarrel is not with an abusive pastor, an arrogant preacher or priest, a coercive church board, or an inflexible representative of the denomination. No, this struggle is rightly waged against principalities and powers, systems and structures of control, liberty-killing oppression, coercion, and manipulation that get in the way of living out a simple faith summarized in the Great Commandment to love God and love our neighbors as we love ourselves.

This struggle, our struggle, is against any and all things—even our religious commitments and biblical interpretations—that prevent us from becoming like Christ; all things that prevent us from showing the mercy and grace of God to others; all things that prevent us from joining Jesus on this journey of merciful discipleship.

If the dog is dead, maybe it *is* better to hear it straight up.

Notes

1. Adapted from Michael LeBoeuf, *How to Win Customers and Keep Them for Life* (New York: Berkley Books, 2000), 35.

2. Matthew includes seven such "woes" in Matthew 23.

3. Landon Saunders, "Night without Vision," sermon, 16–19 September 2007, Abilene Christian University Lecture Series, DVD.

4. Leonard Sweet, *Soul Tsunami* (Grand Rapids: Zondervan, 1999), 34–35.

5. *Merriam Webster's Collegiate Dictionary*, 11th ed. (Springfield IL: Merriam Webster, 2003).

Reflection Questions

1. This chapter is critical of the Pharisees, both ancient and modern. What redeeming qualities do Pharisees or other strict religious groups have?

____

____

____

____

____

2. Do you think Jesus incited the anger of the Pharisees intentionally? Explain.

____

____

____

____

____

3. How does microscopic rule keeping get in the way of doing justice, loving mercy, and walking humbly with God?

____

____

____

____

____

4. I share difficult religious experiences from my childhood in this chapter. Do you have experiences where the good intended by religion turned to poison? How have you dealt with these experiences?

____

____

____

____

____

5. How do you keep from getting angry with individual people and realize instead that principalities and powers—religious structures and systems—perpetuate poisonous injustice?

____

____

____

____

____

Chapter 4

A Fool and His Money

Greed is good. Greed is right. Greed works.
—Gordon Gekko in *Wall Street*

"God, I beg this from you before I die. Give me neither poverty nor riches. Give me just enough to satisfy my needs. For if I grow rich, I may deny you; but if I am too poor, I may steal and insult God's holy name."

So prayed the author of Proverbs 30:8.

This sounds like a "Goldilocks" kind of Proverb. You remember the story. Too hot, too cold, just right, or its variation was the slogan by which Goldilocks lived as she pilfered through the home of the Three Bears. The writer of this proverb would identify with Goldilocks. He needs neither too much nor too little. He needs just enough. But when is enough *enough?* It's hard to say. Getting "enough" is not likely the trouble. Being satisfied with what we have is the sticking point.

More than a century ago, Leo Tolstoy wrote about a greedy farmer in his tale, "How Much Land Does a Man Need?"[1] The farmer was discontent with his life because he never seemed to have enough. He moved from town to town looking for greener pastures and greater opportunities. On his journeys he heard rumors of a faraway place where a distant tribe possessed more land than anyone could walk over in a year, and it was all there for the taking. He went to investigate and found that the rumors were true.

The farmer met with the tribal chief, who informed him that he could in fact have all the land he wanted. He merely had to pay a thousand rubles and begin walking in a circle. Everything within that circle, so long as he completed the circle by sundown, would be his. Early the next morning, the farmer began his greedy acquisition of land. He began running as quickly as he could, trying to make as large a circle as possible. Late in the day he realized his great distance from the starting point and began the desperate return trip.

He ran with all his waning strength back to the beginning of the circle. Just as the sun was setting he arrived, sweating and wheezing. The people cheered and celebrated. Never had anyone acquired so much land in a single day! In joy they bent down to rouse the farmer from his exhaustion. He did not stir. He was dead.

Tolstoy concludes the story by saying, "The farmer's servant picked up a spade and dug a grave and buried him. Six feet from his head to his heels was all he needed."

Tolstoy's story is old, but the man still wrote it a couple of millennia after the time of Jesus. The Galilean carpenter had a story about an insatiable farmer as well. It is found in Luke 12:13-21.

The occasion for this parable is a family dispute. Imagine that: siblings fighting over money. More to the point, two brothers are fighting over an inheritance. While it was customary in the culture of the Near Middle East for the firstborn son to receive two-thirds of his father's estate while the younger sons got what was left, this did not mean everyone was happy with the arrangement. An unnamed man who feels shafted in the aftermath of his father's death shouts from the crowd of followers chasing after Jesus to Jerusalem, "Make my brother share his inheritance with me" (v. 13)!

Maybe this man had indeed been shortchanged. Maybe his brother had taken advantage of him. Maybe he simply wanted more. We know nothing about the worthiness of his request, but he asks Jesus to arbitrate in the matter.

Rabbis often interjected themselves into the affairs of those in their village or synagogue. They sometimes even settled legal disputes between individuals, not only family squabbles. But Jesus isn't your father's rabbi. In our passage, he has no such intention of involving himself in a monetary dispute between blood kin. This is a wise move on his part: it's best not to get in the water while the sharks are feeding. Instead, Jesus does what Jesus does. He tells a story.

> A rich man had a fertile farm that produced fine crops. He said to himself, "What should I do? I don't have room for all my crops." Then he said, "I know! I'll tear down my barns and build bigger ones. Then I'll have room enough to store all my wheat and other goods. And I'll sit back and say to myself, 'My friend, you have enough stored away for years to come. Now take it easy! Eat, drink, and be merry!'"

> But God said to him, "You fool! You will die this very night. Then who will get everything you worked for?"
>
> Yes, a person is a fool to store up earthly wealth but not have a rich relationship with God. (Luke 12:16-21)

The farmer in Jesus' story is more than a farmer. He is a rich landowner, likely with many slaves and sharecroppers. He has wildly succeeded. His barns can no longer hold the bumper crops harvested from his fields. His garage is now too small for all his toys. His bank deposits have exceeded the FDIC insurance limits. His cup runneth over.

What is he to do? Share his outrageous wealth with others? No. Jesus gives us a completely self-centered man (note the reoccurring use of the word "I" in the story) whose only goal is to heap his riches into one huge pile. Unhappy with enough being enough, he chooses instead to build larger barns, to expand his portfolio, to take his stock public.

Satisfaction. Fulfillment. Enough. These words are not found in his vocabulary. One does not keep wealth by resting on his laurels, you know, so this rich farmer reaches for more.

A financial broker took a vacation to Mexico. His outing carried him to a secluded fishing village on the country's western coast. It was a place of peace and tranquility. While strolling on the beach one afternoon, he saw a fisherman coming in to port. This fisherman had caught one of the most beautiful fish the broker had ever seen. He asked the fisherman where he caught the fish.

The fisherman answered, "I have the most perfect fishing spot in the Pacific. I catch a fish like this every morning. Then I go home to my wife and clean the fish at our little villa. In the afternoon we take a siesta and then go visit with our friends at the cantina. In the evening we return home and play with our grandchildren. In the morning I get in my boat and the day starts again. It is a wonderful life."

The broker said to the fisherman, "I think I can help you. If you show me where this fishing spot is, we could hire charter boats and tour guides. They would bring thousands of tourists here each year. The town would grow and expand. People would travel from around the world to see and fish in this beautiful place."

The fisherman was dumbfounded. "Why would I want to do something like that?" he asked.

Unyielding, the broker said, "Well, then you would be a wealthy man! As proprietor you would have more money than you could ever spend. You could live life at your command. You could even retire and move to a small, secluded village. You could fish whenever you wanted. You could spend all your spare time with your wife and friends in your villa, and play with your grandchildren. It would be a wonderful life."

Part of the human condition is being attracted to things that hold little true value. They may sparkle and shine, but they blind us to the real wealth we already hold in our hearts and hands. Such is the failure of the enterprising farmer in Jesus' tale.

As he enlarges his operations, the farmer dies suddenly in the night. He does not live long enough to enjoy the accomplishments of his business expansion. Jesus calls him a fool for this—not necessarily because the man wanted bigger barns, but because he invested his fortune in the wrong place. Upon reaching the top rung of success, the farmer found that he had propped his ladder against the wrong wall. Now it was too late to change a thing.

I can remember growing up as a child of the 1970s, envisioning my life as an adult. The turn of the millennium was coming and, with it, my thirtieth birthday. I thought my life would essentially be over at that point. Thirty was, after all, cane-walking, diaper-donning, false-teeth-wearing *old.* Now, years past that mark, I know thirty is not old at all. While silver has begun to appear in my punkish goatee, I have not yet completely reached the metallic age. You know about the metallic age, don't you? It's when you have gold in your teeth, silver in your hair, and lead in your butt. I'm closer, but I'm not there yet.

Still, there was some truth to my youthful anxiety about life ending at thirty. I have not confirmed this, but a friend told me that once you reach thirty-five years old, you have only five hundred days to live. Let that sink in a second: five hundred days. Based on the average life span of an American, once you reach age thirty-five, subtract the time you are asleep, at work, getting dressed, driving your car—all the necessary but time-consuming acts—and your remaining leisure time is the equivalence of about five hundred days.

A year and a half.

Seventeen months.

Seventy-one weeks.

The Scripture says our lives are but vapors on the wind, here only for a moment. My paternal grandfather told it to me like this: "It seems like it took me longer to get to age eighteen than it did to get from eighteen to eighty." I think he was right. The basic laws of economics apply to more than the price of gasoline. These laws relate to our lives as well. We have a limited supply of time. As a result, that time is incredibly precious, even more so with each passing day. What will we do with it?

It is easy, with limited time, to do what this rich man did: spend it all on ourselves. Cruises, exotic getaways, self-absorbed hobbies, conspicuous consumption, the acquisition of higher and higher piles of stuff, more toys, bigger barns. But is this the best use of the lives and resources we have been given? Jesus answers this question with an emphatic "No!" and challenges us to give up the life of foolish self-investment for the life of being rich in our "relationship with God." Or, as J. B. Phillips translates, we must learn to be "rich where God is concerned."

What does this mean?

Consider the world in which Jesus lived, Luke wrote, and this story was told. Jesus' entire career and earthly ministry was contained within a boiling cauldron of Jewish rebellion and unrest. Ultimately the Jews, fueled by nationalism, zealous religion, and past military successes, staged a national revolt against the occupying Romans. The result was the obliteration of the Jewish state in AD 70. Yet this conflict was as much a civil war as a war of independence. It was a battle of classes with the rich, educated, elite ruling class on the one hand and the poor, marginalized, lower class on the other.

The early first century was incredibly prosperous for Palestine, but the common peasant farmer did not share in these riches. The rich grew richer while the poor only grew poorer. Judean society "rotted from within" because of the imbalance of wealth and social justice.[2] The rich made a fortune off the backs of their tenant farmers, and then, with their windfalls, the landowners and financiers loaned back to these same farmers, at exorbitant interest, the money needed to feed their starving families. It was a brutal cycle that pushed the Jewish peasant beneath the already tentative subsistence level, took more than two-thirds of his income, and violated the Mosaic Law intended to prevent this type of injustice.[3]

Was the rich farmer-landowner in Jesus' parable guilty of this type of injustice? We do not know. But we do know he was an eager participant in the system of injustice. Single-handedly he could not have acquired such wealth without the hard work of tenant farmers, the serving class, or even a field full of slaves. Further, even if he was completely innocent of taking advantage of those in his employment, he let greed blind him to the society-crippling needs around him. Not once did he think of his poor fellow citizens, of the plight of the orphans who wished to glean the leftovers from his harvested fields, of the trampled farmer who spent all his days pulling the rich grain from the Palestinian soil to fill the rich man's barn but had no means to put that grain into his children's growling stomachs.

If this rich man was not guilty of overt injustice, he was guilty of self-indulgence, and there is not much difference between the two. This man was a fool because he did not respond to the needs of those around him when he had the means to do so. He was unconcerned for his neighbor and thus bankrupt in relation to God. He was poor in his relationship with God because he treated those around him poorly. This is the revolutionary message of Jesus' parable.

What then does this parable about recognizing and resisting self-centeredness say to those of us living as wealthy American Christians in the twenty-first century? What does it say to those of us who follow the One who had no place to lay his head, when our combined incomes—the income of American Christians—exceeds $5 trillion a year? What does it say to a people who spend more money on pet food and weight loss products each year than we give to education, poverty, and health relief organizations combined?[4] What does it say to those of us who buy (and we who produce) $5 billion of Christian products a year, when the largest Christian organization feeding the world's hungry gets less than a quarter of that amount? Are we so selfishly blind that we will spend more than $11 billion a year on plastic surgery, when that same sum would provide a basic education for every child in the world?

As Americans, we can readily accept a gospel that speaks of a God who meets our needs like a spiritualized vending machine, or a God who gives us a gold-plated credit card and a mansion on a hill to match the golden streets upon which we will one day walk. After all, that is the American dream. But we balk at the idea that the gospel is about a missionary God whose invitation for us to live under the rule of Christ is also a call of responsibility to participate in the here-and-now but not-yet-arrived kingdom of God.

Following Jesus is not a call to self-indulgent satisfaction or to join an exclusive club where "membership has its rewards." It is a call to follow Christ on his mission of making all things new, embracing what is wrong with this fallen world, and working by God's power to make it right. We are called to a life of radical living, of being a countercultural people, of being a tribe who will not stop at "loving God and loving our neighbor." Rather, we will love God *by* loving our neighbor, by focusing not on our own comfort but on relieving the distress of the world around us.

This is much more than a "social gospel," whatever critics may mean by that hazy term. This is being "rich where God is concerned," for if our gospel does not change the way we treat people in this current world, we do not understand the gospel at all.

Regrettably, some will protest at this point: "Why put so much emphasis on this current world? God is not overly concerned with people's physical needs, is he? It is their spiritual needs that are important. We should not worry about the suffering of the present world. It is all going to burn anyway. Just do what you can to prevent suffering in the next world. That is what we should be concerned with. The gospel is about eternity, not today."

Or as a missions strategist once coldly told me, "We have no obligation to people's bodies, only their souls."

Those who make this parable exclusively about heaven, hell, or impending judgment at the time of death miss the point. The question Jesus raises here is not, "Will you go to heaven when you die?" If we spiritualize the parable like this, we can keep it safely at arm's length. However, Jesus actually raises questions like these:

What are you doing with the life you have been given?

Will the world be changed because you lived in it?

How did you invest yourself in a godly direction to enrich the world?

Have you used your blessings and means to bring justice and mercy to others?

Do you know that your treatment of those in need is an indication of how you treat God?

We must prepare ourselves to answer this parable and not explain it away. Wrestling with questions different from these is attempting to sidestep the confrontational force of Jesus' words. It is refusing to embrace the whole gospel: that God has come in Christ to redeem everything fallen about humanity—our communal structures that perpetuate greed and injustice; our social policies toward the poor, sick, and dying; our failure to feed the hungry, shelter the homeless, and protect the abused; our bodies *and* our souls.

Responding to these words of Jesus is more than an individual matter, however. Churches, denominations, groups of Christians—all that is left of Western Christendom I suppose—must answer as well. This parable should force the church into unparalleled organizational and systematic change in how it does missions and spends money. Consider the following:

- Americans give more to churches and various religious organizations than any other charitable vehicle, more than $93 billion dollars to some 300,000 churches every year.
- Eighty-five cents out of every dollar given to churches is spent internally.
- Only 2 percent—two cents out of every dollar put in the offering plate—ever makes it out of our country.
- If American churches reallocated the dollars they spend on building construction and maintenance to food and education programs (about $19 billion a year), global starvation and malnutrition would be eliminated in less than a decade.
- American churches could provide clean drinking water and sanitation to every person on the planet with only 15 percent of their annual corporate income.[5]

Ori Brafman and Rod Beckstrom are neither pastors nor theologians. Both are Silicon Valley entrepreneurs, professionally about as far from the pulpit or seminary as one could get. Yet, their insights into organizational and community transformation are invaluable, particularly for we who live in these unprecedented times with unprecedented wealth while the world languishes in unprecedented misery. Their book *The Starfish and the Spider* is a must-read for anyone wrestling with the issues of systematic change, like those above so needed in the Christian church.

Brafman and Beckstrom take a detailed look at the native Apache tribe of what is now the Southwestern United States. The Spanish were unsuccessful in subduing this wild band. The Mexicans likewise failed. At first, the Americans fared no better. For hundreds of years the Apache maintained their independence against all would-be colonizers, threatening American power up to the turn of the twentieth century. Adaptable, decentralized, as fluid as the wind that blew across their deserts, the Apache would not yield. Then the American government gave the Apache tribal leaders, or *Nant'ans*, cows. And everything changed.

Soon, with the buffalo population hunted to extinction, wealth in the form of walking, bawling bovines became the virus that ate away Apache society from the inside out. *Nant'ans* used the cow as a form of reward and punishment to control rather than lead their society. Centralized accountability and rigidity replaced flexibility. The group's eagerness to travel, and thus remain outside the American empire's control, was abandoned for the white man's farm. Being an Apache no longer meant living as a part of the land, owned by creation. Now the Apache had wealth, for they owned cows. It broke their society.[6]

Wealth is not inherently evil, but it is dangerous. Wealth blinds us to the distress of others. Short-sighted, we work to amass our own possessions and protect our individual and ecclesiastical fortunes, trading in a Christ-directed way of life for bigger profits, softer lifestyles, sacred cows, and strategies we proudly call "faithfulness." Whenever I hear the phrase, "We are called to be good stewards," I take it as a code word for building bigger barns. It is usually nothing short of greed, self-preservation, and selfishness.

May we truly see the 1 billion people of the world living in wretched poverty; the 700 million who live in slums and substandard housing; the 500 million on the verge of starvation; the 200 million exploited children working under forced labor in sweat shops; the 93 million reduced to beggary; and the 2.5 billion thirsty for clean water.

How can God not meet us head on if we continue to build larger barns and milk our cows while the world slips into the abyss? Our wealth must be pushed away from us and out into the world where it can serve God and not our profit-loss statements or our monthly financial reports read in the church business meeting. For neither Christians nor the church are an end unto themselves—spiritually or materially—but we are called, as the people of God and imitators of Christ, to bless and serve the world.

In serving others, the church will save itself from becoming nothing more than a spiritualized 501c3 not-for-profit, self-centered corporation, organized for the benefit of donor tax exemption. In the economy of Jesus, only those who serve will be served, and only those who choose to be last shall be made first. Only those who humble themselves and take on the nature of a slave will be exalted to sit in heavenly places. Serving others will remind us of our identity and call us out from this self-absorbed, selfish world to be the people of God on a journey following his Son, Jesus.

In the days following September 11, 2001, reports of the remarkable story of the New York City firefighters in Ladder Company 6 began to circulate. This small group of men entered World Trade Center One after it was struck by the first hijacked plane. They assisted the wounded and the traumatized, working their way up the building's stairwells. On the fifteenth floor, Port Authority Police handed over to them a sixty-year-old bookkeeper named Josephine Harris. She had descended some seventy floors already and was near collapse. The men of Ladder Company 6 and Josephine Harris slowly began to climb down the last few stories. They talked to her about her kids, her grandkids, and her work, anything to keep her moving. But at the fourth floor she could go no further. She had to sit down and rest.

The men of Ladder Company 6 refused to leave her. They sat down with her in the stairwell. It was then that more than a hundred floors of burning steel and concrete began to crash down on top of them. Each one quickly said their prayers and prepared for death. But death did not come. The fourth-floor stairwell of building one was one of only a few places that did not collapse. When they emerged from the rubble a few hours later, they were alive and, for the most part, well.

"You saved our lives," the firefighters told Josephine.

"But you saved mine," Josephine responded.

And it was all true.[7]

This is a wonderful metaphor of how following Christ works. If we press on toward perceived safety, leaving behind the poor and suffering, the exhausted and the spent, we will not escape this world unscathed. We will die as fools. But in finding those in need of material and spiritual grace and offering it to them freely, we find our own souls rescued from selfishness and corruption. In serving others we find ourselves. We discover the reason for our existence: not to be served but to serve, and to give our lives to others just as Jesus did.

William Barclay was right when he said the most dangerous word in the English language is the word "tomorrow."[8] The people in need of this world-changing revolution cannot afford to wait until tomorrow.

Neither can we.

Notes

1. Leo Tolstoy, *How Much Land Does a Man Need? and Other Stories*, trans. Ronald Wilks (New York: London: Penguin, 1993), 96–110.

2. Martin Goodman, "The First Jewish Revolt: Social Conflict and the Problem of Debt," *Journal of Jewish Studies* 33 (1982): 422–34.

3. John Dominic Crossan, *The Historical Jesus* (New York: HarperCollins, 1992), 99, 221.

4. For these and many more heart-wrenching statistics see www.generousgiving.org.

5. Ibid.

6. Ori Brafman and Rod A. Beckstrom, *The Starfish and the Spider* (New York: Penguin, 2006), 151–52.

7. Judith Acosta and Judith Simon Prager, *The Worst Is Over* (San Diego: Jodere Group, 2002), 13–14.

8. William Barclay, *The Parables of Jesus* (Louisville: Westminster John Knox, 1999), 124.

Reflection Questions

1. What is it about our nature that drives us to want more and more? Do we all desire "things" with the same intensity? What accounts for the difference between people?

2. Is Jesus teaching us that we should never save anything for a rainy day? Why or why not?

3. If you knew you only had five hundred days left to live, how would you specifically spend those days?

4. What are the similar injustices found in the economic structure of Jesus' society and within our own? Do Christians have a role to play in correcting these injustices? If so, how?

5. Read again the statistics related to how the American church spends its resources. Is there anything you can do to change these numbers?

____

____

____

____

____

Chapter 5

Whose Side Is God On?

> When the structure of a particular power becomes incorrigible, the most effective way to take responsibility is to refuse to collaborate.
>
> —John Howard Yoder

My father-in-law was born December 7, 1935. He turned six years old on the morning the Japanese Imperial Air Force destroyed the Unites States naval base at Pearl Harbor. As a child, he saw it as a day of expectation. For the rest of his life, it has been a bittersweet day, as he has both celebrated his years and recalled the deaths of so many young American soldiers and sailors. To this day, he reads the books and stories about that "Day of Infamy" and tears pool in his eyes. If you are of his generation, you can likely remember with vivid detail exactly where you were when you heard the news of the attack.

Likewise, my parents were sitting in a high school classroom on a warm November afternoon in 1963 when the principal announced over the public address system the terrible news that President John F. Kennedy had been assassinated in Dallas, Texas. These teenagers, so far removed from the world stage and politics, wept and cried along with the entire nation. They can recall exactly where they were sitting, who sat beside them, the exact time, and even the smells in the air when they heard the news.

On January 28, 1986, I was a high school student spending the day at my grandmother's house. It was a rare snow day in Georgia. There were probably three flakes on the ground, but that was enough to paralyze half the state. I was watching television on her old cabinet set. I had already been outside in the cold once to turn the antenna pole toward Atlanta. Ice prevented the automated dial from working (some younger readers have no idea what I am talking about here).

I had just settled down to watch the space shuttle *Challenger* lift off with Christa McAuliffe, a social studies teacher, on board. Had school been in session, my science class would have watched the launch of America's first civilian into space, so I thought I would watch at home. In her second minute of flight, the *Challenger* exploded over the Atlantic Ocean. All souls on board were lost.

And of course, who among us can remove from our minds the images of burning towers or the concrete dust and ash falling over Manhattan? Only the youngest have no memory of that catastrophe. Where were you when you first heard the news of the 9/11 terrorist attacks? What did you feel? How long did it take for you to get your mind around what was happening on an otherwise beautiful Tuesday morning?

When tragedies like these take place, I find myself asking the question most of us ask: Why? Why here? Why now? Why them? Why do things have to be this way? We can talk about faulty O-rings, imperialism, assassination conspiracies, even the religio-social dynamics that breed terrorism, but these do not fully explain the heartache and injustice in our world. More times than not, there is no answer to these questions.

People frequently use Luke 13:1-9 to bring some kind of meaning to tragedy. I have used it that way myself. Jesus' audience witnessed two national tragedies: first, an act of political violence and mass murder; and second, a terrible accident in which a tower, or part of a construction project, fell and killed those inside or working on it. People brought these events to Jesus, looking for a rationalization behind them. "Why did this happen?" we hear them asking. "What is the meaning of this?"

I do not think we preacher types have been as responsible with this text and the answer Jesus gives as we should. As usual, Jesus' answer is not exactly what we expect.

> About this time Jesus was informed that Pilate had murdered some people from Galilee as they were offering sacrifices at the temple.
>
> "Do you think those Galileans were worse sinners than all the other people from Galilee?" Jesus asked. "Is that why they suffered? Not at all! And you will perish, too, unless you repent of your sins and turn to God. And what about the eighteen people who died when the tower in Siloam fell on them? Were they the worst sinners in Jerusalem? No, and I tell you again that unless you repent, you will perish, too." (Luke 13:1-5)

At this point in his journey Jesus has been teaching on the coming judgment and correctly interpreting the times (see Luke 12:35-59). He has impressed upon his listeners, a great crowd, the importance and urgency of making peace with God, of being prepared. Some of his listeners, capitalizing on the context, introduce what they feel is a prime example of divine judgment. Pilate, the same man who would later preside over the trial of Jesus, had seized a group of worshipers and executed them, no doubt for insurrection against the government.

This event testifies to Pilate's legendary anger and reactionary violence.[1] The imperial government killed Jewish patriots, and some in the crowd deduced that these rebels got what was coming to them. They believed Pilate's actions were nothing more or less than the hand of God at work. These men got what they deserved.

Jesus introduced the second tragedy. A tower in Jerusalem had recently collapsed, killing eighteen people. The falling of this tower, the tower of Siloam, is often viewed as Jesus' introduction of an accident or an "act of God." That is exactly how some in the crowd probably viewed it: as divine retribution for some terrible sin.

"These eighteen must have done something very bad to die in such a miserable way," goes the logic. In both cases, the conclusion of the crowds was likely similar: "People suffer because God is aligned against them. God is not on their side. This is the only explanation behind otherwise inexplicable tragedy."

The Jewish people, building upon much of the Old Testament, held to a theology best described as *lex talionis*: the "law of the talon," or the law of retribution. It was understood that all disasters were associated with personal sin. One's suffering in this life indicated how sinful they were. They believed that the one who violated God's law received certain punishment. Accordingly, those who prospered were righteous and those who suffered were evil.

Following this line of thought, many of Jesus' listeners would conclude that the astronauts on the space shuttle *Challenger* were terrible sinners, and thus they perished. These people would say that those who did not escape the Twin Towers on September 11 were destined for destruction because they were evil. The young sailors who were shot to pieces or drowned on that Sunday morning in 1941 got what they deserved. President Kennedy was shot because he did something awful. If we follow this reasoning to its conclusion, the evil students are the ones slain in school shootings, and the good students get away. It is a shocking, calloused way of thinking.

My family has persisted through the poverty and difficulties of Appalachia for eight generations, borne by a Protestant faith that mixes with

Wesley and Whitfield, Finney and Fundamentalism, Anabaptistism and Southern pride. My parents, influenced by all these, fell hard into the fundamentalist camp. As such, they understood basic rules by which a person should live his or her life. To violate these rules was, in *lex talionis* fashion, to subject oneself to the violence of God.

You may be familiar with some of these rules: no drinking, no smoking, no dancing, no mixed bathing (a prospect that always intrigued my teenage mind), no Sabbath breaking (though we did not actually gather on the Sabbath), no card playing, and absolutely no questioning of religious authority.

Said religious authority was bound up in "the Preacher." The big Baptist and Methodist churches downtown had a pastor. The Presbyterians had a few elders. The one fledgling Catholic parish on the edge of town had a priest. I did not meet a Jew until high school, so I didn't even know what a rabbi was. But in my little ecclesiastical world, we had the Preacher. He was the combined concoction of teacher, prophet, taskmaster, guardian, and enforcer. I am certain he cut his grass in a three-piece suit, wore nothing but black wingtip shoes, had never heard or used a single curse word, and adopted all his children. (Because, after all, having sex with his wife was certainly too "carnal," a word he often used. I still don't know what it means).

The world in which the Preacher lived was black and white with no shades of gray. There were only hard and fast rules. You were in or you were out. If you wanted to know where you stood, you simply asked him. He would tell you, and he used the pulpit to do exactly that. On Sundays he became an inferno of Puritan proportions. Animated, dripping with sweat, almost always discarding his suit coat and loosening his tie, he implored and coerced sinners down the aisle to the mourner's bench.

It usually worked. Someone "repented" most every service, even if it took thirty verses of "Just as I Am" or "I Surrender All" to force the issue. I remember those altar calls as being more than lengthy. They were nerve-rattling wars of attrition. Who would win this night: the Preacher or the sinner? Sometimes I went forward to repent just so the whole thing would end and we could all go home.

It was the Preacher who arrived at Henrietta Egleston Children's Hospital one Saturday afternoon. My younger brother, just turning six months old, had been hospitalized for weeks with a faulty heart valve and a growing laundry list of complications. He had not yet celebrated his first birthday, but already doctors had cracked his chest open like a melon. His kidneys had failed. His lungs had collapsed. A staph infection in his right elbow resulted in the amputation of his arm almost at the shoulder to save his life—a life that hung by a thread.

Sometimes when my twin sister and I, eight years old, visited him in the intensive care unit, the only part of our baby brother's body we could see were his eyes and the soles of his feet. He was covered with tubes, machinery, bandages, and monitoring equipment. But it had been this way almost since the day he was born.

On a cold night months earlier, I first realized something was wrong with him. Late at night I was awakened by the sickening sound of someone gasping to breathe. It was my brother with whom I shared a room. I awakened my parents and in a panic they rushed him to the closest emergency room, forty-five minutes away. More than thirty years later, I still find myself checking on my own children's breathing almost every night.

Needless to say, this was a horrific time for my family, especially my parents. They certainly needed emotional and spiritual support, a pastoral presence. The Preacher arrived on cue, but he was anything but comforting. I was at the hospital the day he visited and within earshot when he said the most awful words to my parents. To paraphrase, he said, "Surely you have committed some terrible sin for God to visit this kind of judgment on you and your family."

Even as a child I was flabbergasted. Why my parents did not take this religious charlatan out back to the woodshed, I do not know. They were too tired, too shocked, or too kind to do so, I suppose. Either that or they actually believed what he said. They left the Preacher's church eventually, but not immediately. Over the years I've concluded that at the time they believed, to some degree, what he said to them that afternoon. This left me with an odd alienation toward my faith and my family as I never accepted those words spoken in the ICU waiting room that April afternoon. Maybe I have spent the last several decades trying to disprove them.

The Preacher's attitude is the retribution principle in action. It's the idea that suffering cannot come from any source except violation of God's commandments. This was the theological conclusion of Jesus' day, and it remains the conclusion of many people today. This is not, however, what Jesus taught.

Twice in this text he says, "No!" He is emphatic that one cannot always equate great suffering with great sin. Generally speaking, those who do the will of God enjoy God's blessing, and those who do not meet God's resistance, even judgment. This is generally true, but we cannot apply it consistently. We do not always know why people suffer. Sometimes people suffer not because they are bad, but because they are good, or are innocently victimized, or for a plethora of other reasons. One cannot generalize suffering, claiming that the good get what is good and the evil get what is evil. Believing this goes against the testimony of Scripture and our own experiences.

The retribution principle, so entrenched in the Jewish mind, was like a good proverb to encourage everyone to do the right thing, but it was not an irrevocable law. Consider a similar idiom from our own language: "Crime doesn't pay." We quote that to our children, and teachers repeat it to their students. Police officers grin as the proverb rolls off their tongues while they slap the cuffs on some criminal, and judges pontificate about it in the courtroom. It is true. Crime does not pay, generally speaking. But there are exceptions to the rule, are there not? Sometimes crime does pay. The list of those who have financially gained through unethical business deals, insider trading, or outright theft is lengthy. Crime can pay quite well, thank you very much.

Jesus rejected any easy-answer conclusion that tragedy is always the result of overt sin on the part of those who suffer. These calamities were not from God. God was not playing some kind of cruel game. Yes, place the blame at the feet of the god of the Preacher, or of popular hardened religion, or the Jewish authorities of the first century, but not the God revealed to us in the person of Jesus.

Granted, Jesus did not tell us why tyrants get to rule over the powerless. He did not tell us why towers fall on the innocent. He did not tell us why unsuspecting astronauts meet a fiery crash, or why some escape the destruction of terrorists' attacks and others do not, or why tornados hop and skip over one home only to land in full force on another. He did not explain the trajectory and path of Atlantic basin hurricanes or why infants spend months of their lives in a children's hospital. He did not go there at all, like some flaming television evangelist explaining famine and tsunamis as the judgment of God. Instead, he followed these two accounts of tragedy with strange words: "Unless you repent, you too will all perish."

This is where the customary interpretation of this passage hits the wall. It is also where, when preaching from this text in the past, I have always stopped my sermon. I did not necessarily want to get into whatever else Jesus was saying. But that is irresponsible, because Jesus *is* saying something else besides the "rain falls on the just and the unjust." He says, "Repent."

Repent? What has repenting got to do with falling towers and blood on the altar, especially after Jesus establishes the fact that these events are not necessarily the result of God's judgment? Jesus is not one to waste words, and Luke is not one to fail in recording what he wants us to hear. So let's dig a little deeper.

Pilate's violence, in this particular case, is likely related to the construction of an aqueduct needed to alleviate Jerusalem's water shortage. It was a public works project to get water into the city that took place in close proximity to the timing of Jesus' ministry. That sounds harmless enough, but Pilate had raided the temple treasury to pay for the project. The priests administered the treasury funds and always set aside money for the infrastructure needs of the city. These funds were at the Roman governor's discretionary use because Rome was the occupying power of the Middle East.

Pilate's mistake is that he over reached. Either through violence, coercion, or intimidation, he took both the discretionary fund *and* the "holy" money reserved for temple use only.[2] This led to an open rebellion of sorts, something to which Pilate was accustomed. He had to quell more than thirty major riots in his decade of Roman service in Jerusalem, and his "peacekeeping" almost always led to bloodshed. The incident in the temple, since the temple treasury was the cause of the trouble, was likely the aftermath of this particular rebellion. Pilate had retaliated against and executed those he saw as insurrectionists, those whom many of the Jews considered patriots. He then mixed their blood with the temple sacrifices in an atrocious act of sacrilege.

Those who introduced this subject did so for a reason. While no fan of Pilate, from their perspective, these Galileans were on the "wrong side." This is the reason the tragedy befell them. If God were pleased with them, if they had lived right, then their rebellion would have succeeded. God would have blessed their jihad as in olden days. If the participants had actually been holy enough, things would have worked out differently. So the question is put to Jesus, "Did these patriots, or insurrectionists, die because they were sinful?"

The questioners attempted to pull Jesus into a political discussion. Many of the common folks and Jewish aristocracy held the idea that "since we can't beat them," speaking of the Romans, "we might as well as join them." They used this event as validation of their conclusion. "God is on our side, the side of political expediency," they said. "Look what happens to those who rebel against Rome."

Then Jesus played devil's advocate, introducing not the story of a random tower falling on eighteen innocent civilians, but the other side of the equation. "Yes, the patriots/insurrections died in their efforts to throw off Roman oppression. They were murdered in the temple. God must not be on their side. But what about the eighteen killed by the falling tower of Siloam?" It is likely that these eighteen victims of the tower's falling were actually working on the aqueduct system being built with the stolen money from the temple.

A master at playing verbal cat and mouse, Jesus is saying, "God was not on the side of our patriot countrymen who were killed in their insurrection against Rome. So he must be on the side of the collaborators, the ones willing to cooperate with the Romans. No, wait a minute! Those who died in this tower accident were our countrymen too. They did not rebel against Rome. In fact, they took the stolen temple money, went to work for the enemy, and profited as a result. Which of these two groups are the worse sinners, the freedom fighters or the collaborators?"

Jesus, not so delicately, challenges his listeners: "Pick your team. Pick up the sword and fight the empire. Wage holy war. Try, by force, to throw off the oppression of Rome. Or let them pay you off. Become a partner with Caesar. Compromise and negotiate. Name your price, whatever it is, and make a deal. Decide which side you think God is on."

It is not happenstance that these were the two leading options in Israel at the time on how to deal with the Roman Empire. Even the religious parties were divided: kill or cooperate; wage war or compromise; take up the tools of violent confrontation or the slithery means of political accommodation. Which would it be? Jesus says, "Neither." Consider what is behind door number 3, a door labeled, "Repent."

"Unless you repent, you will perish, too. Both the jihadists and the compromisers are going to lose in the end," Jesus says. "If you follow either of these paths, you will all die as a result. Fight the empire or capitulate to the empire. It will be the end of you all."

When Jesus used the word "repent," it was not in a privatized way, like an angry revivalist preaching at a camp meeting who says, "Give up your lying, cheating, stealing, whoring, drinking, and smoking. You need to get religion. You need to join the church. You need to improve your morals."

Instead, Jesus, in telling them to repent, is saying, "You must give up your agenda for living in this world, and your plans for the future, and trust me to bring you a tomorrow. Abandon these crazy ideas of yours, where you think the right combination of religious piety, or the right political play, or the most deftly played insurrection, or the right Caesar in Rome will bring you peace.[3] None of these will bring you the kingdom of God. Only I can bring that kingdom to bear. Repent of believing anything less than that. Change your mind, and trust me that I am telling you the truth. Killing and/or compromising are both dead-end streets because neither of these are the path to the kingdom of God. Follow me instead."

The day came a mere thirty years after these words were spoken when blood did flow in the streets of Jerusalem and in the temple. The day came when the Romans tore down every tower and wall because these very hearers did *not* repent. They chose a path that rejected Christ. They refused to align themselves under the rule of the kingdom of heaven and walk the path to the City of God. They attempted to bring the kingdom of God in by force, with politicians and religionists and the business end of a sword. Rome, the imperial superpower of the world, met this rebellion with unmerciful force, and the end was exactly what Jesus had prophesied.

To refuse the way of Christ and take up the tactics and tools of the world is to guarantee corporate and individual disaster—in the first century and, yes, even today.

Driving the point painfully home, Jesus uses, of all things, a fig tree. This mini-parable immediately follows the discussion of bloody sacrifices and falling towers.

> Then Jesus told this story: "A man planted a fig tree in his garden and came again and again to see if there was any fruit on it, but he was always disappointed. Finally, he said to his gardener, 'I've waited three years, and there hasn't been a single fig! Cut it down. It's just taking up space in the garden.'
>
> "The gardener answered, 'Sir, give it one more chance. Leave it another year, and I'll give it special attention and plenty of fertilizer. If we get figs next year, fine. If not, then you can cut it down.'" (Luke 13:6-9)

The owner of a garden goes out to pick fruit from one of his fig trees. This is not a wild blackberry bush growing along the side of the road or down a row of fence. This is an intentionally planted tree, in cultivated soil, but there is no fruit. In Palestine it would take about three years for a fig tree to reach maturity, the time mentioned in the parable and, incidentally, the length of Jesus' ministry. Once mature, the tree would bear fruit about ten months out of the year. Only in the late spring would the tree be bare.[4]

In frustration the owner of the vineyard says to his servant, "Just cut the tree down. It is unproductive. It has leaves. It is green. It gives a little shade. It looks like a fig tree. It walks like a fig tree. It talks like a fig tree, but this fig tree has no fruit. It is just taking up space. Get rid of it."

In Jewish literature, the people of God are often portrayed as a fig tree (see Isa 5; Jer 24; Ezek 31; Hos 9; Joel 1; Matt 21; Mark 11; among other places). Jesus invokes familiar language for his listeners, providing context once again for a radical message. God has come to his people, time and time again, looking for the fruit of repentance, looking for them to be what he has created and cultivated them to be, and he has always left disappointed. His people continually chase after lesser things. They always go looking for self-created solutions to their problems.

They look like faithful people. They sound like spiritual people. They have their Scriptures and the temple, but there is no fruit. They do not bear the marks of the distinct people of God. They operate by the policies of the world, singing the song and dancing the dance of the powers that be, allowing the world's rules of engagement to dictate what comes next, and in that there is no future for the people of God.

It is important to note in this parable, just as it is important to note Jesus' response to martyred worshipers and falling towers, that God is not the sender of these violent outcomes. Did God "get them" because they were evil or did something terribly wrong? Absolutely not. Jesus' warning is, "Make sure you don't 'get yourself' with your own rebellious actions, bad decisions, and stubbornness. Quit trying to figure out whose side God is on, and make sure you are on God's side!"

God does not directly have anything to do with so many of the things we suffer. We do it to ourselves because he was never a factor in the equation—we didn't even consult or consider God in the first place! This is not a parable about God destroying people. It is a parable about finding redemption from our own self-destruction.[5]

Look at the gracious appeal Jesus makes here as the servant of God. He says, "Give me a little more time. Give it one more chance. I will work the soil. I will spread fertilizer. I will water the roots. I will give this tree of God every chance and then some." The owner of the field relents and agrees. For all this talk of violence and judgment, in the end, this parable is about grace. Jesus keeps working our soil. Jesus keeps plowing close to the roots. Jesus keeps the pressure on us as we writhe about in the fire of his words and actions. He keeps jabbing and punching, not letting us squirm off the hook. Why? Because he loves us, he knows what we can become, and he recognizes that we often need to be saved from ourselves.

Move from this parable to the end of Luke 13, just a few more verses, and Jesus completes his thought with an invitation. On his way to Jerusalem, with a broken heart he cries out, "O Jerusalem, Jerusalem, the city that kills the prophets and stones God's messengers! How often I have wanted to gather your children together as a hen protects her chicks beneath her wings, but you wouldn't let me" (v. 34). Jesus pleads with, begs, and works the soil of those journeying with him to Jerusalem. This is the merciful message of Luke 13.

My son Bryce and I had an episode recently. He and I have a lot of episodes. You see, Bryce thinks I am too hard on him, that I pick on him too much. You know what? He is right. I am tough on him.

He and I were at loggerheads the other morning. It was time for him to catch the bus and we were going over our daily litany: brush your teeth, find your book bag, get your homework off the table, take your medicine, put on your shoes. He was frustrated, and so was I. Before we knew it, we were in a screaming match.

I never understood the possibility of child abuse until I had a child. God, how is it that a nine-year-old can drive an otherwise rational, self-controlled adult into a raging animal in need of a tranquilizer?

Anyway, there we were, fully engaged. I could hear the bus in the distance and Bryce was sitting in the hallway crying in his underwear.

"Stop messing with me!" he cried. "You're always messing with me!"

Then, in one of those moments where we say what is right in spite of ourselves, I said, "Yes, I am messing with you. And you'd better pray that I keep messing with you. As long as I am messing with you it means I love you, I believe in you, and I am doing all I can to make you what you can be."

Did Bryce get it? I don't know.

Do we get it?

Luke sketches for us a Jerusalem-bound Jesus who offers us the invitation to

- align ourselves under his Lordship,
- come into the kingdom of God,
- gain a new understanding of reality,

• discover anew who God is.

He challenges us to give up on our stubborn personal, social, and religious inventions, which will only lead to disaster.

"Come, follow me instead," he says. "Repent. Give up your agendas and your wrecked ways of thinking and trust me to give you peace, to give you salvation, to give you a future."

I believe he will keep messing with us until we get it.

Notes

1. Josephus, *Antiquities* 18.3.2.

2. Susan Sorek, "Render Unto Caesar? Pilate's Acquisition of Temple Funds," 7 January 2003, online at http://arts.monash.edu.au/publications/eras/edition-4/sorek.php (accessed 12 February 2008).

3. N. T. Wright, *The Challenge of Jesus* (Downers Grove: Intervarsity Press, 1999), 43–45.

4. William Barclay, *The Parables of Jesus* (Louisville: Westminster John Knox, 1999), 127.

5. David Wenham, *The Parables of Jesus* (Downers Grove IL: Intervarsity Press, 1989), 198.

Reflection Questions

1. What sort of inexplicable tragedies—personal, national, or otherwise—cause you to wonder about God's actions or lack of action in the world? How do we reconcile our belief that God is over all things, yet injustices seem to pile up daily?

2. Do you believe in *lex talionis*—the law of retribution—as explained in this chapter? Why or why not?

3. Jesus frames the Jewish response to empire and power along three lines: fight, compromise, or repent. Do these options apply to Christians living in America? Explain your answer.

4. Which is the more pressing hazard: that God will "get us" or that we will "get ourselves"? Why?

5. Do you think Christ is "messing" with his church today? If so, how?

____

____

____

____

____

Chapter 6

Who Could Blame Him?

> You have to understand, most of these people are so inured, so hopelessly dependent on the system, they will fight to protect it.
>
> —Morpheus from *The Matrix*

"That was one hell of a sermon, preacher."

So went the word of encouragement passed on to my good friend at the conclusion of an especially inspiring Sunday morning sermon. The young man paying the compliment was a diesel mechanic named Terry. Terry came to church every Sunday with grease still under his fingernails, tattoos peeking out from beneath his cut-off sleeves, and his best tattered jeans hugging his hips. Of course this did not mean Terry failed to recognize a good sermon when he heard one, even if his praise was a bit unorthodox.

Beaming from ear to ear, pumping the pastor's hand, the young man was happy to attend this little church to hear good sermons and pursue his new-found relationship with Christ. It had not always been so. Terry's story is one of glorious conversion, like something you'd hear at a Billy Graham crusade. Drug abuse, alcoholism, failed relationships: he had suffered from and caused more than his fair share of disaster. Then, by God's grace, it all turned around. Terry came running to Christ.

My friend, his pastor, was instrumental in the transformation. He served as a spiritual guide to Terry, helping him sort out his past baggage, pointing him forward, and allowing the rough edges to remain. After all, God looks at a person's heart, not the grease under his fingernails. If only people could do the same.

One Wednesday evening, Terry was running late for the church's weekly Bible study. He came straight from work. No shower, no shave, no change of clothes. He came like that old hymn we often sing: "Just as I Am." A self-appointed delegation met Terry in the parking lot on this particular night. The group told Terry that should he wish to continue to be a part of the church, it was time he learned to dress right, cover those devilish tattoos, and clean up his language.

Terry's reaction was expected. He was crushed. Bible in hand, he returned to his truck, drove away, and never came back. The chances of him giving church another shot are slim to none. Who could blame him?

My friend discovered the wrongdoing against Terry after the fact, when Terry's usual seat in worship was inexplicably vacant. To his credit, my friend no longer pastors that church.

Question: Why won't some people go to church?

Answer: Because they have been to church.

Jesus intentionally broke the rules and customs of the religious establishment of his day, not for the sake of rebellion, but to reveal how preposterous it was to hold to meaningless rules. Strict legalism that misses the point of God's grace and freedom in Christ is more than preposterous. It is grotesquely sinful.

This journey of Jesus now takes us into the Jewish synagogue, the heart of the religious establishment. This stop along the way is actually two stops in one. The following events involve Jesus' healing of the sick on the Sabbath day in the witness of Israel's religious leadership. These are recorded in Luke 13:10-17 and 14:1-6:

> One Sabbath day as Jesus was teaching in a synagogue, he saw a woman who had been crippled by an evil spirit. She had been bent double for eighteen years and was unable to stand up straight. When Jesus saw her, he called her over and said, "Dear woman, you are healed of your sickness!" Then he touched her, and instantly she could stand straight. How she praised God!
>
> But the leader in charge of the synagogue was indignant that Jesus had healed her on the Sabbath day. "There are six days of the week for working," he said to the crowd. "Come on those days to be healed, not on the Sabbath."
>
> But the Lord replied, "You hypocrites! Each of you works on the Sabbath day! Don't you untie your ox or your donkey from its stall on the Sabbath and lead it out for water? This dear woman, a daughter of Abraham, has been held in bondage by Satan for eighteen years. Isn't it right that she be released, even on the Sabbath?"
>
> This shamed his enemies, but all the people rejoiced at the wonderful things he did. (Luke 13:10-17)

> One Sabbath day Jesus went to eat dinner in the home of a leader of the Pharisees, and the people were watching him closely. There was a man there whose arms and legs were swollen. Jesus asked the Pharisees and experts in religious law, "Is it permitted in the law to heal people on the Sabbath day, or not?" When they refused to answer, Jesus touched the sick man and healed him and sent him away. Then he turned to them and said, "Which of you doesn't work on the Sabbath? If your son or your cow falls into a pit, don't you rush to get him out?" Again they could not answer. (Luke 14:1-6)

These two Sabbath healings are directly related, not only because they occur on the Sabbath and not only because they are both contained within the Great Journey of Jesus. Luke ties them together like a double helix to reinforce Jesus' growing controversy with the religious establishment.

First, Jesus is in the synagogue and spontaneously heals a crippled woman, inciting a rebuke from the synagogue leader. We will return to this incident shortly. Then, days later, Jesus is invited to eat with the religious leaders on the Sabbath day. The dinner party is a direct result of the previous synagogue healing, for it is not a social gathering. It is a trap.

"Let us get this Nazarene to ourselves, away from the Sabbath crowds," the religious leaders say to each other, "and we will see if he breaks the Sabbath laws once again."

To add to the drama, an unlikely guest attends the dinner party: a man with swollen extremities. The King James Version calls it "dropsy," and our word is "edema." No doubt this man is placed at the table as a pawn. He is bait, thrown out by the Pharisees to see if Jesus will act in private as he does in public. It is one thing to break the Sabbath in a faraway synagogue with an excitable crowd as the backdrop. It is another thing to break the Sabbath in the presence and under the pressure of the religious and academic leadership.

"Surely this Jesus is not fool enough to do it again?" they think. "We will test him privately, for we cannot risk another public fiasco. If he behaves appropriately, we will keep our eyes on this young fellow. If he acts inappropriately, well, we will know for certain that he is a menace who must be dealt with accordingly."

Jesus does not disappoint, of course, revealing his compassionate consistency for the sick in public as well as in private. He is not manipulated or power-played into conformity by this ad hoc collection of inquisitors. He boldly takes their bait, heals the suffering man, and turns their religious nitpicking back on their own heads. But the real bombshell is the synagogue episode. We return to it now.

Jesus attended synagogue on the Sabbath day, something many faithful Jews did each week. Since there was only one Jewish temple, many miles away in Jerusalem, the synagogue was the gathering place for worship, ritual, and instruction for the rank-and-file members of Israeli society. The synagogue followed a distinct order of worship with well-established rules.

The practice of following an ordered liturgy is not unlike the average Protestant or Evangelical attending Sunday services at a local church. Even in the free-group churches of my childhood where we did not have written orders of worship, we knew what was appropriate and inappropriate. In those churches, having a preset order of worship, even a sermon title, was an act of heresy that quenched the Holy Spirit's freedom. Still, we all knew the order of events, even the exact moment when old Mr. Scott would commence to shouting hallelujahs on the third verse of "Amazing Grace." These traditions were not written down, but they never changed.

For Jews living in the first century, however, the Sabbath involved much more than synagogue attendance and familiar unspoken expectations. I would like to say it involved much less, as God intended that the Sabbath be a day of worship, rest, and renewal. But by the time of Jesus, it had become a heavy weight, and it was nearly impossible for the average worshiper to keep up with all the rules.

As an example, consider the prophet Jeremiah. In his day, the keeping of the Sabbath had broken down to the point that it was indistinguishable from any other day of the week. Caravans, shop-keepers, money-changers, and the like paraded through the streets of Jerusalem taking advantage of those religiously required to make sacrifices at the temple. Sabbath day in ancient Jerusalem looked like the parking lot at Wal-Mart on the day after Thanksgiving.

Jeremiah cried out in protest, "This is what the LORD says: Be careful not to carry a load on the Sabbath day or bring it through the gates of Jerusalem. Do not bring a load out of your houses or do any work on the Sabbath, but keep the Sabbath day holy, as I commanded your forefathers" (Jer 17:21-22, NIV). Breaking the Sabbath, in light of the prophet's warnings and in the aftermath of Jerusalem's destruction by its enemies, became one of the more substantial sins the religious authorities attempted to regulate. To stave off God's future wrath, the Pharisees and experts in the law implemented a strict code of obligations regarding the Sabbath. In fact, the

Talmud, the Jewish book providing commentary on the Mosaic Law, prohibited thirty-nine different categories of Sabbath activity, ranging from writing any more than two letters of the alphabet to tying one's shoes. Once the academy fully expounded upon these categories, the result was a nexus of hundreds if not thousands of outlawed Sabbath activities.

This was a far cry from the Exodus commandment or Jeremiah's warning to "remember the Sabbath and keep it holy." In an attempt to regulate people's work, the Pharisees turned the Sabbath day into more work than the average struggling Jewish family could possibly complete.

On a particular Sabbath morning as recorded in Luke 13, Jesus sits in this milieu of legalism. There, across the synagogue, is a crippled woman bent double by affliction. His heart goes out to her. With just a word and a touch, he makes her well. This is no smoke-and-mirror trickery of a traveling tent-meeting evangelist. This is the Messianic power of God. Fittingly, the woman explodes with praise to God, for after eighteen years of suffering, she is free. The crowd likewise is astonished. But not everyone is happy with this turn of events. The leader of the synagogue explodes as well, but in rage.

Allow me to bring this story forward: Imagine you are seated in church on a Sunday morning. It is your church, the one with which you are familiar, the one you have attended for many years. It is a good Sunday as far as worship services go. You were tempted to play golf or sleep in, but there you sit as faithful as ever. The church is three-quarters full. The worship leader is doing his usual dance of weaving the old hymns with the modern worship choruses to keep everybody semi-content. It's not too bad.

The children's feature was entertaining enough. The Cooper kid blurted out another embarrassing revelation about his mother in front of the whole congregation. It got a good laugh and a few red cheeks. The Miller family has packed their pew in front of you, as is their custom. Across the aisle sit Mr. and Mrs. Walsh. Mr. Walsh is the one who gets there early to open the doors and turn on the lights and the air conditioning, and he is the one who stays late to lock things up. Mrs. Walsh is always patient and gracious as she waits for him, even though her osteoporosis has all but broken her in half. She has shrunk to no more than five feet tall. Those Walshes are salt-of-the-earth people.

Standing for the offertory and the doxology, you see an unfamiliar young man seated in front of you. He wears a faded and frayed plaid shirt, old khaki pants, and Wolverine work boots. He is short but looks lean and strong. His hairline is receding a bit and his face bears a three-day beard. You notice he has eyes of fire—kind and compassionate eyes—but like fire nonetheless. He has several friends seated with him, including the Gardner brothers who used to live one street over from your house.

As the pastor rises to deliver his sermon, the young man rises as well. He walks directly to where Mrs. Walsh sits. With a smile he whispers something in her ear, gently touches her shoulder, and returns to his pew. Suddenly, like lightning striking, old Mrs. Walsh stands up, as straight as a string, as tall and fit as she was thirty years ago. The congregation erupts with wonder and thanksgiving! Mrs. Walsh shouts for joy as her husband, his cheeks wet with tears, hugs the young stranger. Mouths fall open. Eyes bulge from their sockets. Miss Juliet Palmer nearly faints.

Then, from the pulpit, the pastor calls the whole place to order. His face is scarlet with anger. His eyes flash. He looks down at the young, smiling, wonder-working intruder as if he could grind him between his teeth.

"This is the Lord's house," he booms across the sanctuary, "and this is the Lord's Day. You will not turn it into a spectacle with your parlor tricks."

You and the congregation hold your breath and look to the young man in the Wolverines for what comes next.

Maybe this modern story helps us understand the explosive nature of Jesus' confrontation in the synagogue.

Eighteen years—eighteen years!—this woman has suffered. Once she is healed, the synagogue leader (insert: pastor, elder, chairperson of the church board) can only fret over the minutiae of keeping the rules! He cannot celebrate with everyone else the physical and spiritual deliverance of one who has long suffered. He can only see the grease under the fingernails of a Nazarene carpenter who has violated the sacred customs.

He tenders the most audacious rebuke: "There are six days of the week to get healed—not on the Sabbath." In other words, "Don't bring your sicknesses and illnesses, your addictions and demons, your problems and long-borne burdens in here. Leave those outside. It is good for people to get well, but not on Sunday and not in the church house. Don't violate God's law by healing on the Sabbath."

Jesus responds with a rebuke of his own, calling the leader of the synagogue and anyone who agrees with him a hypocrite. With no compassion for the suffering, these religious leaders violate more than the spirit of God's law; they violate God's people.

Landon Saunders is correct when he says, "Get it right about people and the rituals, religion, Scriptures, and doctrines might get right. But get it wrong with people and everything else will be wrong."[1]

This is Jesus' exact point. A religious system whose rules and traditions are more motivating and more powerful than its compassion for people is a system of hypocrisy. When more time, energy, and resources are spent on enforcing religious conformity and statutes than are spent on caring for and reaching out to the suffering, then the crimes of the ancient Jewish synagogue have been propelled forward into the twenty-first century, and the fuming words of Jesus are hurled off the page, as fresh and relevant as they day they were first spoken.

When "doctrinal integrity" (a term usually defined by those using it) trumps kindness and grace, faith has wandered out of bounds. Anything claiming to be truth that does not lead to compassion for our neighbors cannot rightfully be called the truth.

My friend Susie is a good nurse. She is professional, skilled, and tough. If something can take place within the constricted space of a hospital room, she has probably seen it, and not much rattles her. Like many in the medical profession, she has acquired the emotional defense mechanisms necessary to continue the care of the sick. But Susie is not as hard as stone, not always, anyway. Beneath her medicinal bravado lies a soft side. She is deeply moved by the sufferings of the ill. She has wept with the families of the dying. She has held the hands of more than one confused, anxious patient.

When her work overwhelms her, Susie does what is natural. She searches for deeper meaning in all the misery surrounding her. Involving yourself in the sufferings of others is stifling. You have to escape at times just to breathe.

Susie was on an escape some time ago and found herself in the most unusual place: church. See, Susie gave up on organized religion a long, long time ago. But there she was sitting in a worship service, looking for something. Actually, she was doing more than sitting and looking; she began to participate. She found herself singing the songs of praise, devoting herself to prayer, and giving herself completely to those precious moments. She then did what many of us have done. She went down the aisle of the church to pray at the altar.

Susie was met with great empathy and compassion as she knelt, prayed, and cried, filled to capacity by the Spirit. But then things changed. She was removed from the sanctuary and shuffled to a back room for additional "counsel." A woman sat down in front of her, knees close enough to touch

Susie's, and with a clipboard began to work through an exhaustive checklist. The list included everything that would now be required of Susie based on the "decision" she was making: weekly attendance requirements, financial expectations, church allegiance, assignment to a mentor.

Upon hearing all this, Susie seemed to feel God's presence drip from the ends of her toes. She regained her emotional toughness and promptly told the woman sitting across from her that she was not interested in any of those things. The woman put her clipboard away, folded her arms, looked at Susie, and said, "If you turn back now, your decision tonight won't mean anything. You could leave this place, die in a car accident, and go straight to hell."

Susie told her counselor to go there first.

What Susie needed in those moments was understanding and gentleness. She needed others to pray with her, to love her, and to stay out of the way of what God was doing. She did not need a visit from the equivalent of a used-car salesman explaining the fine print of a proposed contract.

Susie has never returned to a church sanctuary. Who could blame her?

The church can become dangerously underhanded, dehumanizing the people we are called to serve. The fractured though beautiful creations of God are reduced to donors who can put dollars in the offering plate, heresy-prone sheep who must be kept on a short leash, cogs in the denominational wheel, and numbers on the roll. Even those of us charged with leading the church do not often notice that we do this to people. How can we when we spend the lion's share of our time oiling the squeaky wheels of our congregations, attending unending committee and denominational meetings, maintaining the organizational machinery, and keeping up our church's market share in the community?

Meanwhile, compassion for the least of these is lost as he or she is sucked into the conformity-driven, well-managed, faceless mob. To this Jesus could not submit, and neither should we.

But miniscule, compassionless rule-keeping is not the only issue on the table on this particular Sabbath day. Jesus' acts of healing, both public and private, were certainly acts of compassion that honored the spirit of Sabbath—for every day is the right day to do the right thing. They were also acts of intentional exposure, revealing the absurdity of religious rules. But more so, these were acts of authority.

Jesus purposefully performed these acts on the Sabbath day to take back from the religious system the power it had abused and did not deserve. Jesus seized the authority held so tightly by the religious leaders and ripped it from their hands. Jesus, as the Messiah of God, had arrived to storm the religious Bastille, to put things right, to confiscate the territory these impostors had taken from a compassionate God, and to topple the religious machine from its pedestal.

Jesus was neither a nonconformist nor a reformer with the ambition of improving the existing system. He did not come to tinker with the machinery. He came to substitute something else in its place. Nor was Jesus a simple rule-breaker, for the woods are full of that animal. Jesus was not even a heretic. Heretics, while often dangerous to the status quo, can be marginalized or made into ranting fools well enough. No, this wild-eyed, self-made rabbi from Nazareth was a challenger. He had come to takeover. The angry reaction was thus more than theological road rage over being cut off on the spiritual highway by a reckless driver. It was much deeper.

Jesus threatened to steal their followers with his revolutionary message. Jesus sought to undermine their "God-given" and traditionally accepted authority. Jesus, if allowed to continue, would prove to be the downfall of the entire religious system, if not the society that was built upon it. To their credit and most contemporary Christians' shame, the religious leaders of Jesus' day quickly recognized the sweeping implications of his ministry.

At the conclusion of the Sermon on the Mount, there is a sometimes overlooked ending. In Matthew 7:28-29 we read, "When Jesus had finished saying these things, the crowds were amazed at his teaching, for he taught with *real authority* [emphasis added]—quite unlike their teachers of religious law."

We can safely assume that this was the common conclusion wherever people encountered Jesus, for here in Luke 13 the crowds are quickly won over as well (v. 17). While the religious establishment was blind to those who needed compassion, they were not blind to this One who undermined their authority. They could see clearly enough that the people actually *believed* Jesus. And of course, if Jesus was telling the truth it meant they were not telling the truth. He was a dangerous man indeed.

Manipulation, threats of divine retribution, the micromanaging of people's lives and morality, judgmentalism, paranoid insecurities, obnoxious self-righteousness: we can lay all these crimes at the feet of many of Christianity's proponents, from the Roman Curia to the most protesting of Protestants. Yet, all of these are mere symptoms of a deeper illness. As Jesus said, the real sickness is hypocrisy.

Much of Christianity (and its leaders, I might add) is more concerned with protecting its position and power than caring for people. As such, it suffers from a crisis of credibility: it offers a false image of the God it represents. Granted, we can bring our individual and collective beliefs and practices under the lordship of Christ, and we who call ourselves Christians should do exactly that. But we must be quick to accept that even something we label "Christian" or "Christianity," if it is not submissive to the words and ways of Christ, must be recognized for what it is: a damnable lie. Even Christianity can become idolatry.

Is there any other conclusion to which we can come when

- there are churches that subjugate and marginalize women while Jesus treated them with nothing but equality and scandalous respect?
- theological constructions have been manufactured that enable and encourage Christians to treat the world like a toilet that we will soon leave behind, yet Jesus taught that the kingdom of God was both now and coming to earth?
- we justify the continued ignoring of the poor while Jesus said acts of mercy to these and the marginalized is a direct act of service toward him?
- we sort people into baskets—the good and the bad, the elect and the damned, the heaven-sent and the hell-bound—when Jesus showed clearly that such judgments are for God alone to make, and even then God's grace trumps the worst of sins?
- hateful campaigns are waged by the church against those we despise for their social and sexual transgressions, while these are the very people with whom Jesus would associate?

Again, Jesus came to reform *nothing*. He came to set the world on fire. This realization, that following Jesus and practicing Christianity are not always identical, turns up the heat on those of us who have done our religion's heavy lifting over the years. But when confronted by this Jesus, are we willing to change our conclusions about faith, about what it means to be Christian, about what it means to be "saved," about most everything we have built our lives around and upon? Are we willing to change our minds? If we cannot change our minds, we cannot change anything.

Change is hard, especially for Christians. We are about as inflexible a species as they come. Certainly, many of the faithful are all too happy with this assessment, equating rigidity with orthodoxy. I'm not so sure about that.

Consider our friend Galileo. Do you remember him from your middle school science class? This father of modern astronomy was one of the first to propose a sun-centered galaxy. The earth, he said, revolves around the sun, not the other way around. This got Galileo in gobs of trouble.

The church, you see, took the Bible literally back in the seventeenth century, and the Bible says, "The world cannot be moved" (Ps 93; 95; 104). So, pitched against the Bible, the pope, and Christendom, Galileo and his telescope were put on trial for heresy. After the inquisition, his research was condemned as unorthodox, his books were refused publication, and he was sentenced to prison, though later the punishment was commuted to house arrest. It could have been much worse had Galileo, under threat of his life, not recanted.

Things finally worked out for Galileo. On All Saints Day, 1992, Pope John Paul II finally gave in, admitting that yes, the earth does in fact rotate around the sun and the interpretation of the church for some three centuries was—gasp!—wrong.

Facing truths that do not fit into the framework of *our* truth, *our* "biblical worldview," is nothing new, not in Jesus' or Galileo's day, and not in our own. What do we do when we encounter such truth? Typically, we reject it. We refuse all things that do not suit our perspective, labeling it sacrilege, just as the religious leaders in Jesus' day did. Do not misunderstand me. I am not one who thinks that one truth is as good as another as long as sincerity is involved. I define truth not as a bullet list of talking points, drafted and adopted statements, or even age-old creeds. Truth is a person, Jesus, and we must pursue him.

Still, most of us in the Jesus camp tend to think that truth is locked in a dusty footlocker and stuffed underneath the church altar. It is a fixed, hard as stone list of propositions without adjustment, no matter what Galileo's telescope or anybody else's research says.

Let me explain. Do you ever use a vacuum? If you do, I bet you have done this: You are gliding across the living room carpet busting dust mites when your trusted Hoover encounters a fuzz ball it cannot conquer. What do you do? You pick up the fuzz ball. You roll it in your fingers. You inspect it as closely as possible. Then, inconceivably, you do what we all do: you put it back on the carpet and run the vacuum over it again and again and again with the same failed result.

We do the equivalent when encountering a truth—or even an image of Jesus—that does not fit our theological view of the world. We stop, pick him up, inspect him, and then persist, in failure, to make him fit. We never stop to consider that we cannot get the job done with the equipment we have always used. The problem is not the novel revelation we have encountered. The problem is our stubborn resistance to reconsider what we believe or to view those beliefs from a different angle. The problem is admitting that the truth, or even the perspective of Jesus to which we have held so tightly and for so long, may not be true after all.

We embrace some beliefs only because they are the official party line. Or we often believe what we do because it is what we have been told to believe. Or we come to our personal conclusions because that smiling preacher on television or behind a pulpit told us it is the truth. That is not enough.

Granted, this can be frightening. Launch into an examination of all that is locked away in that musty church locker and you might get accosted by the establishment. Start assailing the flawless truths of your church and you may find yourself seated next to Galileo at a heresy trial or next to Jesus at a Pharisaic dinner of inquisition. But do not be afraid. Truth can take it, at least those truths worth holding on to. Anything that cannot take it should be discarded anyway.

By the way, after this dual encounter with his nation's religious leaders, we never find Jesus attending the synagogue services again.[2] Never.

Who could blame him?

Notes

1. Landon Saunders, "Night without Vision," sermon, 16–19 September 2007, Abilene Christian University Lecture Series, DVD.

2. Leon Morris, *Luke,* rev. ed., Tyndale New Testament Commentaries (Grand Rapids: Eerdmans, 1995), 244.

Reflection Questions

1. The Pharisees attempted to do the right thing—keep the Sabbath—by writing and enforcing more and more rules. Does this work? Why or why not?

2. When someone experiences Christ outside the establishment's accepted way, why can some people not bring themselves to celebrate?

3. Which is more important: doctrinal integrity or compassion for others? Explain.

4. Why do you think Jesus is a threat to religious systems? Are all religious systems threatened by Jesus? Why or why not?

5. I say that "even Christianity can become idolatry." How is this possible? Is rigidity the same thing as orthodoxy?

____

____

____

____

____

Chapter 7

The Gospel according to Gatorade

> The Mississippi River will always have its own way. No engineering skill can persuade it to do otherwise.
>
> —Mark Twain

I have no way of testing the following proposition, but Malcolm Gladwell says it is true. Gladwell is the author of the best-selling book *The Tipping Point: How Little Things Can Make a Big Difference.* Gladwell proposes this mental exercise: Take a large piece of paper. Fold it over in half. Then do it again, and again, and again, until you have folded that paper fifty times. When finished, how tall do you think the final folded piece of paper will be?

The size of a phone book?

As thick as a mattress?

As tall as a refrigerator?

Gladwell says the folded piece of paper would be as high as the distance from the earth to the sun, with only fifty folds. This is what mathematicians call "geometric progression." Something that starts incredibly small, when it doubles upon itself, takes very little time to become something extraordinarily huge.[1]

My father used to play a game with me when I was a boy that illustrates this same point. He would say, "What if I had four flat tires on my car, and I offered to pay you to change them all for me. Which would you rather have: $10,000 or a dollar for the first lug nut, but I'll double it every lug nut thereafter?"

I would always take the $10,000 and he would chuckle but never explain anything to me. I was much older before I realized that if I took the doubling dollar, at the end of the tire-changing session I would have much more than $10,000. So if you ever come across someone on the side of the road who happens to have four flat tires and makes such an offer, don't take the lump sum.

Do you believe little things matter? Sure you do. And more than paper folds and lug nuts. Microprocessors in our computers, antibodies in our bloodstreams, the placement of a single decimal point or added zero on our bank statements, a single vote in a toss-up election. Oh yes, we believe little things matter.

In Luke 13, Jesus tells two little parables about two little things to describe the kingdom of God he is bringing to the world. "Wiki-wiki" is the Hawaiian word for "quick," as web sites like Wikipedia and Wikianswer prove. Here Jesus tells quick stories, wiki-parables. He throws out two wiki-descriptions of the kingdom of God. What these descriptions lack in words, however, Jesus makes up for in meaning and implication for you and me who now live in the kingdom of God established by Jesus.

> Then Jesus said, "What is the kingdom of God like? How can I illustrate it? It is like a tiny mustard seed that a man planted in a garden; it grows and becomes a tree, and the birds make nests in its branches." He also asked, "What else is the kingdom of God like? It is like the yeast a woman used in making bread. Even though she put only a little yeast in three measures of flour, it permeated every part of the dough." (Luke 13:18-21)

The mustard seed is a familiar image in the Gospels. Jesus said if we have faith the size of a mustard seed, it is enough to move mountains (see Matt 17:20). Here, Jesus reaches for that tiny little seed once again and compares it to the kingdom of God. Jesus says the kingdom of God begins as something small; a mustard seed is only a millimeter in diameter, yet it grows into something extraordinary, something large. A domesticated Palestinian mustard plant, miniscule in its beginning, could grow into a bush or tree that was more than seven feet tall. The kingdom of God grows like a piece of paper folded fifty times or like your money when you take the dollar-a-lug-nut option.

If Jesus were here today, telling his stories and yarns and reaching for pictures that describe the kingdom of God, he might reach for something else, since few of us grow mustard. Our experience with the herb is usually restricted to squeezing yellow sauce on a hot dog.

"To what shall I compare the kingdom of God?" Jesus might ask today. "It is like the Mississippi River."

The headwater of the Mississippi River is not what you might expect. Flowing out of a glacial lake in the frozen tundra of northern Minnesota is a small rivulet. This stream is so narrow and shallow that one can walk across it with water reaching only to his or her knees. But a drop of water flowing out of that lake begins a journey that will carry it more than two thousand miles through the heart of North America to the Gulf of Mexico. And that is not the only drop to make the journey.

For instance, if you go hiking in western New York and a drop of your perspiration hits the ground, that drop will find its way to the Mississippi River and the Gulf of Mexico. If you drop your water bottle while camping in the Grand Teton Mountains of Idaho, those droplets will find the Missouri River, then the Mississippi, and finally the Gulf of Mexico. With more than twenty major tributaries, the Mississippi River Basin sustains with its water and commerce more than fifty percent of the American population. The center of this country would be a desert without it. By the time the Big Muddy reaches Louisiana, it is 3 miles wide, 200 feet deep, and moving the mass of 150 tractor trailer loads of water every second.

As the spring rains show us most every year, levees, dams, sandbags, and the wherewithal of the U.S. Army Corps of Engineers is not enough to tame Old Man River. When the Mississippi River rages, nothing can stop it. But in Minnesota, children can play in it as if it were a mud puddle.

That is the exponential growth Jesus describes as the movement of God in the world: like little drops coming together to form a trickle, then a stream, then a mighty river; like a mustard seed planted in the ground and then springing up, growing, spreading, and reaching for the sky. The kingdom of God may begin in a subtle, undercover fashion, but it will explode into the world, flooding and overtaking it.

What is this kingdom of God of which Jesus speaks? Yes, it is like a mustard seed. It is like yeast worked into flour. To use our modern parable, it is like the growing Mississippi River, but what is "it"? What is this kingdom?

We find the phrase "kingdom of God" or the equivalent "kingdom of heaven" on Jesus' lips more than a hundred times in the Gospels. It was his favorite subject. If we were forced to sift Jesus' message and preaching down to one idea, this would be it: "The kingdom of God is at hand." Though it cannot be reduced to a single theme, the best way to understand this kingdom speak is to see it as God's nation. It is the territory over which God reigns.

George Eldon Ladd summarizes the kingdom of God like this: "The Kingdom of God is the redemptive reign of God . . . his rule among human beings. This kingdom, which will appear at the end of the age, has already come into human history in the person and mission of Jesus to overcome evil, to deliver people from its power, and to bring them into the blessing of God's reign."[2]

God has come to his creation in the person of his anointed Son, Jesus of Nazareth, whom he vindicated by raising him from the dead. God is now ruling the world through this Jesus, a rule of compassion and justice that will put the world to rights. It is a rule that is in the here and now, and it is a rule that is still coming. It is present today in our midst and in our hearts, and it has yet to arrive completely. It has begun, but it is not yet complete.

Just as that trickle out of the frozen tundra of Minnesota can rightfully be called the Mississippi River, it is not the end of the Mississippi River. A mustard seedling, as it first bursts through the soil, can be called a mustard tree, but it is not yet fully grown. When sealed in a jar, yeast is fermented and fermenting, but it is not complete until it is freed to consume the entire lump of dough. So it is with the reign of Christ and the kingdom of God. It is here and now, announced and begun as Jesus journeyed toward Jerusalem, and it is still in process.

His rule has begun in our hearts and in our communities of faith, yet in hope we look forward to the time when that reign will extend over all creation. By faith we anticipate the day when God finally and ultimately makes Jesus Christ ruler over all and all in all. To live in this kingdom of God is to live in the future; it is to live in the truth that Jesus already reigns, for his reign has begun in us.

I am no huge science fiction fan, but I will never forget the storyline of the first *Terminator* movie starring Arnold Schwarzenegger. I was a teenager when the movie first hit the big screen, and it was bigger and scarier than life. The basic plot of the movie, and others similar to it, goes like this: A being from the future travels back in time to affect, alter, or change the future. If you did not like *Terminator*, then think of Michael J. Fox in *Back to the Future* and you have the same effect.

In such movies, what happened to the people living in the present when they realized what the future would look like? What did it do to them? It changed the way they lived in the present! They cast aside the meaningless, the worrisome, and the trivial. Faced with what the future held, they began to concentrate on the things that would matter when the future became reality. They began to align their lives to match what was coming. "If the world is going to look like *X*," they said, "then I must begin to live like *X*." They became future-oriented people in the here and now.

When Jesus came announcing that the kingdom of God was at hand, and when he implemented that kingdom through his death and resurrection, he was serving notice as to what the future was going to look like. Not to push the analogy too far, but like a time traveler, he reached into the past and into our present, and he yanked them into the future. He said, "This is what God's new world will look like. This is what God's kingdom is and will be. I will serve as the compassionate, just, redemptive Lord over all. My people, those who follow me in the journey of faith, will begin to live that way *today*, as if the future is already here, for genuinely it is. They will give their lives to me and live under my rule in the present, anticipating when that rule will extend over everything."

We get the shot, today, to live as if the mustard tree is fully grown, giving shade, shelter, and comfort to those who come underneath its limbs. We can live today as if the river already rolls through the countryside. We can live today as if the yeast has already devoured the loaf. That is what the future will look like, so we must live as if that future has already come.

Certainly we understand that people still need food. People still fight wars. People still tolerate injustice. Spiritual darkness and hardness of hearts still abound. There is suffering, anxiety, evil, and grief. But where God's reign through Christ is acknowledged, we know that the kingdom is gaining momentum. Little drops turn into big drops. Tributaries and rivulets collapse on top of one another. The basin of God's power draws everything to itself until finally this river brings life to the whole world. The tree will finally grow up, and that motivates us to meet these challenges head on, for the future will have no hunger, war, or injustice. We live, not ignoring these present realities, but working hard to bring them into alignment with the future.

But that is not all the mustard seed and yeast tell us. As usual with Jesus, there is more here than meets the eye and ear.

Mustard was an important herb in biblical days. It had culinary uses, of course, as people used it to make dressings, flavor food, and season meats. It also had medicinal value. Mustard could be used to treat respiratory troubles or made into a liniment, an ancient version of Ben Gay for sore joints and muscles.

Mustard was abundant and grew wildly all over Palestine. In fact, it was often a nuisance. Like an ever-growing weed or winding crabgrass, mustard tended to take over anywhere it went. It destroyed fields and crops, sprouting through the soil in less than a week after the seed hit the ground.

Still, Jewish farmers did not want to be rid of it completely. A domesticated and cultivated variety of mustard was brought into the garden, as in Jesus' parable. It was essentially the same plant, but had been somewhat tamed. It had to be watched, though. If not carefully managed, it too could break lose and overrun a garden as quickly as its wild brother.

The point Jesus makes is not only that this kingdom of God is something that starts small and ends big—which is usually as far as we take the parable—but that the growth of this kingdom has intrusive, takeover qualities.[3] A mustard seed could not leave well enough alone. It overgrew and consumed everything around it. This is the exact quality Jesus ascribes to the kingdom of God. If we think we are going to contain or quarantine the kingdom of God, then we had best think again.

This mini-parable poses an unsettling challenge, then. We want just enough of the kingdom to bring a little flavor to our lives, or for medicinal purposes we will take enough of Jesus to fetch us comfort when we have no other options. But Jesus does not spring into action like a pill poured out of a bottle or a genie steaming from a lamp. Jesus is not here to spice up our lives. He has come to take over our fields. To take Christ into our well-ordered, well-kept lives is in many ways to ask for trouble, for he will not leave well enough alone. He will not let us have our own way or be content until his rule in and over our lives is complete. Our careers, our children, our possessions, our churches, our checkbooks, our hearts, our minds, our imaginations, our past failures, our futures, our plans, our worries, our ambitions: he wants it all, and he will not rest until he has it.

Thus, people will resist this kingdom, even as those Jesus encountered on his way to Jerusalem resisted it. Religious organizations and structures who find this Jesus too forward and unmanageable will resist it; church leaders who must maintain their command and control over people rather than giving that role to Christ will resist it; individuals who cling to supervising their lives and the lives of others and dictating their own personal agendas will resist it. Every effort will be made to keep Jesus in the corner of the garden.

"Yes, I will take Jesus in small therapeutic doses to help me through, or better, leave him out there in the future. I will trust him to take me to heaven when I die. Call him when that time comes, and he can hold my hand as we journey toward the light together, but do not mess around with my life today. Jesus can have my soul, but I will maintain power over my life."

Sorry. You do not get one without the other.

Resist it. Plow around it. Fence it in. Burn it back. Pull it up. Spray over it. The kingdom of God will still overrun our well-manicured, well-managed, well-protected lives like kudzu set loose in a field. We cannot stop it.

The second parable connects to the first. The kingdom of God is "like the yeast a woman used in making bread. Even though she put only a little yeast in three measures of flour, it permeated every part of the dough" (v. 21).

The bakers and brew-masters of Egypt, five thousand years ago, stumbled upon yeast and were the first to use it in the kitchen. While in use for ages, the reasons yeast works have only been realized in the last two centuries. Louis Pasteur, of gallon milk fame, finally figured out the science of it all in the mid-1800s when he discovered, and this is wonderful in light of Jesus' words, that yeast is alive. It is a living organism. Searching for life, the yeast cell breaks down and boils the starch in flour, producing sugar. Then the enzymes in the yeast go to work on the sugar, feeding upon it further and producing carbon dioxide. This is what puts bubbles and fluffy air holes in the dough and makes bread rise. A byproduct of this process is also alcohol. Fermented beer and fluffy bread: yeast is essential to both of these.

In days gone by, certainly in the day Jesus spoke, one did not go out and buy yeast in a can or a foil wrapper. A baker had to make his own. We can still make our own yeast today, since odorless, tasteless one-cell yeast fungi float all around us. Just mix flour and water together and let it sit for a week or so. One day you will notice that it smells bad and has bubbles in it. Yeast cells have landed in your little flour gumbo, and it is fermenting. After a few more days it will smell good, or at least better, and you can begin to add it to flour and water to make your bread rise. Warning: Please do not follow this exact recipe unless you want your entire family to be treated for food poisoning. But you get the idea.

Jesus was not invoking the scientific, technical aspects of yeast in this parable. His listeners had no idea about such things. They simply knew that if you put yeast in a mixture of flour and water, it made bread rise. It transformed hard, tasteless tack into something light and delicious. In Jesus' parable, a small amount of yeast is enough, he says, to ferment a large amount of flour. It will make enough bread to feed scores of people.

These two wiki-parables say the same thing. Yeast, like mustard, is a sign and symbol of the kingdom of God. Both have takeover qualities. With yeast, something from the outside, something subversive and microscopic but very much alive, finds its way into the bland, dead, and tasteless to transform it. Like enzymes breaking down the starches and the sugars, Christ will have to break down our resistance, the lives we have lived, the power of our own schemes and religiosity; but once he enters our lives, nothing can stop him from having his way. And when he has his way, the final product is far better, far superior to what we have had or known.

With this in mind, take a few steps forward with Jesus on his journey as we go to Luke 17. There Jesus says something else about the kingdom of God that we cannot ignore.

> Once, having been asked by the Pharisees when the kingdom of God would come, Jesus replied, "The kingdom of God does not come with your careful observation, nor will people say, 'Here it is,' or 'There it is,' because the kingdom of God is within you." (Luke 17:20-21 NIV)

Our ever-present, friendly neighborhood Pharisees come to Jesus with a question: "This kingdom that you speak of, the reign of God, when will it come?"

I do not think the Pharisees were open to Jesus' message; this journey has proven that much. But they were interested in the kingdom of God. The Jews living in Jesus' day prayed for God's kingdom to come. They prayed for the breaking of the bondage of Roman oppression. They prayed and longed for the day when all their problems would be solved, their liberties restored, their suffered injustices made right, and their needs met. They wanted nothing more than for God, through his Messiah, to extend his rule of justice and peace over the entire world. Jerusalem would serve as the capital city and they would share divine power with the Christ.

I cannot fault their mindset because I too long for that kingdom to come. I long for the day when there will be no more injustice, no more pictures of maimed and bullet-ridden soldiers, no more hungry children, no more school shootings, no more battered wives, no more drug addictions, a day when the television has no reports of bloodshed, fear, rape, chemical spills, or mourning widows. I too wait for the day when all of God's people will live at peace with Christ as the gracious ruler of creation. I want the future of which we have only a taste to come rushing into the present. I pray as Christ taught us to pray: "Thy kingdom come," and with the Apostle John I say, "Even so, come Lord Jesus." I ask the same question, "When will the kingdom come?"

There is a bit of danger, I'm afraid, in asking this question. It is possible, in our anticipation of the future kingdom, that we become so distracted by some hoped-for rescue that we miss the kingdom today. We Christians are super obsessed with discerning the signs of the times, with reading the theological and eschatological tea leaves, with arranging our doctrinal systems and posting our end-times outlines. We hang on the words of those who postulate what will happen when this particular Middle Eastern country does this or that, or if a particular candidate gets elected to a particular office, or if war breaks out in a specific corner of the world.

We have charts and conferences and series of books and preachers with massive apocalyptic display boards behind them as they preach. We even have terribly made movies about these things, including third-rate actors and such cheesy scripts that they belong in a Velveeta box. Thousands of good people—God's people—swallow this as if it were gospel truth rather than a fairly contemporary and very Western interpretation of the obscure Jewish prophets.

Consider that there are some three hundred direct Messianic prophecies concerning the first coming of the Christ in the Old Testament.[4] Yet when Jesus was born in Bethlehem, not the first priest, preacher, scholar, theologian, seminary professor, televangelist, or Bible student was there to greet him. The Jewish interpretation of messiah was so out of pace with Jesus' birth and subsequent ministry that they could only reject him. They missed him because their expectations and God's reality never came together. Their interpretations and doctrinal systems were wrong. With four thousand years of divine inspiration and communal history to guide them, they could not get it right.

Are we so arrogant to think we will get it right the second time? Hardly. It is a waste of time and energy to speculate on such things. It is a waste of the days we have been given. Jesus says so.

"The kingdom of God does not come with your careful observation," Jesus said. We cannot predict the day and the hour. We cannot develop, interpret, and decipher some ironclad apocalyptic code. Our projected calendar is wrong. Why? Because whatever date we pick in the future and whatever sequence of events we follow will be wrong, for the kingdom is not out there somewhere. The kingdom of God is within is. It is in our midst. It is here. It is now. Christ has already come. God's rule of justice and peace begins today, if we will have it. To look for the kingdom of God only in the future is to miss the responsibility and privilege of living under Christ's rule today.

Dr. Robert Cade and Dr. Dana Shires, both of the University of Florida, are responsible for one of the greatest inventions of the previous century. It was not the computer chip, the television set, or the Internet, but it was and remains a technologic breakthrough. In 1965 the coaching staff of the University of Florida came to the two professors needing help with hydrating their players. In the swampy humidity of central Florida, these athletes' biggest challenge was staying on their feet. Drs. Cade and Shires invented a lemon-lime electrolyte-filled drink that they affectionately named after the University of Florida football team: Gatorade.

Gatorade is the most researched sports drink in the world and has spawned an entire market of look-alikes and wannabes over the past forty years. Gatorade has hydrated millions of amateur and professional athletes including spokespersons Tiger Woods, Derek Jeter, Peyton Manning, Mia Hamm, Michael Jordon, and, of course, most of you who are reading this book. I have never lived a day without Gatorade being a product on the market, and hardly a week without it being in my body.

Gatorade's marketing pitch for the last decade is as genius as their product. We see in their television ads or printed images an athlete exerting himself, sweating profusely: lifting weights, kicking a soccer ball, hanging from the rim of a basketball goal, swinging at a baseball. Huge drops of Gatorade-colored perspiration trickle off his skin, and the question is asked: "Is it in you?"

The implication is clear. You cannot succeed, you cannot win, you cannot even compete unless you have the right stuff in you. Of course the right stuff is Gatorade, now available in eighty countries and in more than two dozen unique flavors.

Here is the same question for you and me: Is it in you?

Has the rule and reign of God through Jesus found a home in your heart? If it has, then it will not stay in you. It will ooze out. Great drops of God's reign will rain on the community and the world around you. For the nature of this kingdom is to overgrow the field in which it is planted. It leavens and changes the entire mass of what it encounters. It cannot leave well enough alone.

How can we with any integrity pray for God's kingdom to come and not live wholeheartedly as citizens of that kingdom today? Could it be that we ask God to do something in the future in which he expects us to participate in the present?

Rather than sitting in cramped Sunday school rooms hopelessly trying to figure out what is next on God's apocalyptic calendar, and rather than shaking our heads and condemning the world and what is wrong with it, wouldn't our time and neighbors be better served if we labored to advance God's current and coming kingdom rather than living as if the world is already dead?

We have a role in this great story that is the kingdom of God, this journey to which Christ has called us. In the greatest act of grace short of the cross itself, God has given us a part to play in the redemption of creation. His good pleasure is, amazingly, to do his will and work through us.

When you wipe the tears off the cheek of a crying child, the kingdom comes. When you feed the hungry in the name of Christ, the reign of God begins. When you offer shelter to a battered woman, the seeds are planted. When you show kindness to your neighbor, the yeast mixes into the dough. When you stand up against injustice and right a wrong, God's nation expands. When you direct a person out of poverty and indignity, you inject the antibiotic of God's grace into creation.

When you lead a person to the hope and redemption found in Christ, the kingdom of God takes root in the world.

In the small, insignificant actions you may not think twice about, and truly, in actions no one else may notice, God does his best work. Singing a song, preaching a sermon, painting on a canvas or a wall, conducting honest business dealings, caring for patients in a hospital, waiting tables, serving food and drink, building a house: all these acts—and a million more like them—echo in eternity. All these things matter when we do them with Jesus as our Lord, for that is living in the future *today*.

The consuming kingdom of God is found in you and through you. It is breaking in. It is invading this world, and though not yet complete, it has begun. Your invitation is to be a part of it today.

This is not some enlightenment-driven or self-improvement save-the-world program. This is not an individualistic approach that believes God will awaken the secret spark that burns in every human heart if only we look for it. No, this is something other, something outside of us, something foreign and holy but life giving, that moves in and devours our beings and shows us a new way to live. We do not have to find it (remember the "Here it is" or "There it is" counsel of Jesus [Luke 17:20-21]). We only have to surrender to it.

Imagine that a freewheeling young man meets a young woman, and he sees that she is a beautiful, marvelous creature. He says to himself, "I like being single, but if I was going to marry someone, that is the kind of woman I would marry."

If his heart led the way, they would wed immediately. But impulsive emotions do not always lead the way. The young man's brain wakes up and says, "Slow down, pal! You'd better get to know this person before you jump in head and heart first. You don't know what you are getting into."

So he takes some time to learn more about her. He spends days and weeks with her, and in the end discovers that his emotions were correct. This is a woman to whom he can give and entrust his heart. Still, there is not a wedding. Not yet. Before he meets her at the altar he must answer this question: "Am I willing to give up the life I have, the life I am now living, for a new life with this person?" Only in the surrender to this new life does a wedding take place.

Following Jesus on this journey of faith into the kingdom of God is no different. It is more than an emotional response. It is more than a deep attraction born out of much time learning his words and ways. It is surrender, a giving over of the life we have for a life with him.

The decisive question of the kingdom of God is not, "Where is it?" for it is wherever Christ reigns. The better kingdom question is, "How do I get in on it?" The undeniable answer is Jesus. He is the essence of this kingdom of God and the one to whom every knee will one day bow and of whom every tongue will one day joyously confess that he is Lord.

That is the future. That is today. That is the kingdom of God. Is it in you?

Notes

1. Malcolm Gladwell, *The Tipping Point: How Little Things Can Make a Big Difference* (New York: Back Bay Books, 2002), 11.

2. George Eldon Ladd, *A Theology of the New Testament,* rev. ed. (Grand Rapids: Eerdmans, 1993), 89–90.

3. John Dominic Crossan, *The Historical Jesus* (New York: HarperCollins, 1992), 278–79.

4. Josh McDowell, *The New Evidence that Demands a Verdict* (Nashville: Thomas Nelson, 1999), 164, 201.

Reflection Questions

1. How would you describe the kingdom of God to someone who had never heard of it? Do you think Christians really understand the kingdom of God?

2. At times the world looks empty of anything resembling God's kingdom. How can we explain this? Why does it seem this way?

3. In what little ways has the kingdom of God begun to overtake your life, your church, your family, your work, your world?

4. Are there dangers of being obsessed with the timing of the future or the second coming of Christ?

5. What role do we have to play—if any—in bringing the kingdom of God to bear in the world today?

____

____

____

____

____

Chapter 8

Brides, Birthdays, Baptists, and Born Again

> Until the Last Day comes, we must not despair of anyone's salvation, but must long and pray for the reconciliation of all without exception.
>
> —Timothy Ware

On a clear day I could look across the valley in which I grew up and see mountains in all directions: To the north, I saw the rising and falling crinkles of the Cohutta wilderness that includes Grassy and Fort Mountains. To the west lay the Armuchee Ridges with Johns and Horn mountains and the occasional glimpse at the backside of Lookout Mountain. To the south stood mountains with names like Red Top and Cass. To the east were the Appalachians, the closest peaks being Pine Log, and Ryo. I could not possibly name every mountaintop I saw from the porch of my childhood home. There are too many. But I could spot and recognize the prominent peaks.

This journey of Jesus is long, with many peaks and valleys. It covers nine chapters, fourteen or so parables, three dozen changes of subjects, and some four hundred individual verses. A book the size of an encyclopedia would still offer only a glance at the prominent peaks. So while our view of this journey is not complete, it is still beautifully striking.

One of the more remarkable high points is what English Bibles call "The Great Banquet," "The Parable of the Great Banquet," or "The Story of the Dinner Party." This is my favorite of Jesus' parables. While it is not as well known as the story of the Good Samaritan and does not have the raw emotional power of the tale of the Prodigal Son, it is the most radical story Jesus tells. In this parable, Jesus throws out of the kingdom, the party of God, the very ones we would expect to find there. The ones we would never expect fill their now-vacant seats at the table. It is a great reversal of position and status where godless outcasts, society's untouchables, and barefaced oddballs gather.

These people who wander in off the street uncombed and unshaven, smelling like body odor, cheap wine, and urine, who do not know the difference between a salad fork and an hors d'oeuvre, and who have no clue about table manners or cocktail party etiquette are made the guests of honor.

Meanwhile, those who have enjoyed favored status for their entire lives, who have lived at the upper echelons of society because of their birth, their wealth, their religious piety, their class superiority, or their political connections, find themselves outside on the street. Suddenly, the elite eat out of trashcans. They scramble to find their next meal. They try to fight off the cold of night with newspaper blankets and barrel fires.

This reversal takes place not because the master of the feast, obviously God in Jesus' story, hates the blue-blooded fortunate of society. It takes place because the fortunate refuse the invitation to come to the party. This party will be celebrated with or without those initially invited. This party is for all who will enter the door, even those who do not know where the door is.

The explanation of this parable is obvious: While there is no room in religious structures and ecclesiastical systems for outsiders who will not keep the rules, God goes out of his way to find these rule-breaking outsiders and invites them in as family, for he has plenty of room in his house and in his heart for the least of these.

I will not belabor the minor details of this parable, but the implications of Jesus' words here are another story. Maybe we can best flesh out the repercussions of Jesus' words in the form of a few additional stories. If we grasp the world-shattering message of Jesus here, we might begin to realize the far-reaching grace of God. We might allow that grace to reshape our ideas about what it means to be the people of God. And we might have to learn to live with the tension that the story of God's gracious salvation is nothing short of an outrageous scandal.

Kyle Paxman is a beautiful, smart, young woman just past her thirtieth birthday. A couple of years ago, not only was she busy with her career, managing her food and beverage businesses in Carlsbad, California, but she was also busy planning her wedding. Her dress was fitted. The flowers were ordered. The menu for the reception was finalized. Scores of guests confirmed their attendance at the event and prepared to travel from all over the United States to the Basin Harbor Club in Lake Champlain, Vermont. Then disaster struck.

Six weeks before Kyle's scheduled wedding, a young man, a stranger she had never met, walked into her office. He possessed a collection of e-mail messages and other evidence that revealed Ms. Paxman's fiancé was cheating on her. And the stranger should know: his own girlfriend was the other guilty party.

What to do?

Initially, the jilted bride and her mother began canceling reservations and events associated with the wedding like the rehearsal dinner and reception. They discovered, however, that they would never be able to recover all the money they had spent, for the deposits were nonrefundable. Daughter and mother began to think of creative ways they might put the items to good use and in the process make something positive out of something terrible.

Ms. Paxman and her parents invited 125 women, only a few of whom were among the original invitees, to enjoy cocktails and a four-course dinner as a fundraiser to help the underprivileged. Rather than bringing wedding gifts, the new invitations said, "Bring your checkbook." They chose the Vermont Children's Aid Society and CARE USA as the designated charities.

The Vermont Children's Aid Society offers child-centered social services including adoption, pregnancy and family counseling, and birth-parent support services. Kyle had supported agencies like the March of Dimes in the past, and since the party was planned for Vermont, this seemed like a good match.

While she and her mom mulled over other possibilities, a television advertisement for CARE USA snagged their attention. CARE is a humanitarian organization that focuses on working alongside poor women. When equipped with the proper resources, women have the power to help whole families and entire communities escape poverty. CARE works to improve basic education, prevent the spread of HIV, increase access to clean water and sanitation, and deliver emergency aid to survivors of war and natural disasters. What could be better? CARE became Kyle Paxman's other charity of choice.

The people at CARE said Kyle Paxman's plans were some of the most unusual they had ever encountered. Unusual or not, they worked. Kyle's fundraiser garnered a total of $10,000 for CARE, which she dedicated to a program to build educational and job opportunities for families in Bolivia so they would not have to send their children to work in the local zinc mines. Her story has inspired dozens of other substantial donations, and after the event, Kyle and her mother enjoyed a vacation to Tahiti, formerly the honeymoon trip she had planned.[1]

The kingdom of God is nothing less than Kyle Paxman. This is the turning-on-its-ear power of Jesus' parable of the Great Banquet. It embraces and welcomes the downtrodden, the poor, and the forgotten, while the former guests of honor sit on the sidelines.

Tony Campolo relates an experience he had late one night in Hawaii. I share it here in its entirety. He says,

> Up a side street I found a little place that was still open. I went in, took a seat on one of the stools at the counter, and waited to be served. This was one of those sleazy places that deserves the name, "greasy spoon." I did not even touch the menu. I was afraid that if I opened the thing something gruesome would crawl out. But it was the only place I could find. The fat guy behind the counter came over and asked me, "What d'ya want?" I said I wanted a cup of coffee and a donut. He poured a cup of coffee, wiped his grimy hand on his smudged apron, and then he grabbed a donut off the shelf behind him. I'm a realist. I know that in the back room of that restaurant, donuts are probably dropped on the floor and kicked around. But when everything is out front where I could see it, I really would have appreciated it if he had used a pair of tongs and placed the donut on some wax paper.
>
> As I sat there munching on my donut and sipping my coffee at 3:30 in the morning, the door of the diner suddenly swung open and, to my discomfort, in marched eight or nine provocative and boisterous prostitutes. It was a small place, and they sat on either side of me. Their talk was loud and crude. I felt completely out of place and was just about to make my getaway when I overheard the woman beside me say, "Tomorrow's my birthday. I'm going to be 39."
>
> Her friend responded in a nasty tone, "So what do you want from me? A birthday party? What do you want? Ya want me to get you a cake and sing 'Happy Birthday'?"
>
> "Come on," said the woman sitting next to me. "Why do you have to be so mean? I was just telling you, that's all. Why do you have to put me down? I was just telling you it was my birthday. I don't want anything from you. I mean, why should you give me a birthday party? I've never had a birthday party in my whole life. Why should I have one now?"

When I heard that, I made a decision. I sat and waited until the women had left. Then I called over the fat guy behind the counter, and I asked him, "Do they come in here every night?"

"Yeah!" he answered.

"The one right next to me, does she come here every night?"

"Yeah!" he said. "That's Agnes. Yeah, she comes in here every night. Why d'ya wanta know?"

"Because I heard her say that tomorrow is her birthday," I told him. "What do you say you and I do something about that? What do you think about us throwing a birthday party for her right here tomorrow night?"

A . . . smile slowly crossed his chubby cheeks, and he answered with measured delight, "That's great! I like it! That's a great idea!" Calling to his wife, who did the cooking in the back room, he shouted, "Hey! Come out here! This guy's got a great idea. Tomorrow's Agnes's birthday. This guy wants us to go in with him and throw a birthday party for her right here tomorrow night!"

His wife came out of the back room all bright and smiley. She said, "That's wonderful! You know Agnes is one of those people who is really nice and kind, and nobody does anything nice and kind for her."

"Look," I told them, "if it's okay with you, I'll get back here tomorrow morning about 2:30 and decorate the place. I'll even get a birthday cake!"

"No way," said Harry (that was his name). "The birthday cake's my thing. I'll make the cake."

At 2:30 the next morning, I was back at the diner. I had picked up some crepe-paper decorations at the store and had made a sign out of big pieces of cardboard that read, "Happy Birthday, Agnes!" I decorated the diner from one end to the other. I had that diner looking good. The woman who did the cooking must have gotten the word out on the street, because by 3:15 every prostitute in Honolulu was in the place. It was wall-to-wall prostitutes and me! At 3:30 on the dot, the door of the diner swung open, and in came Agnes and her friend. I had everybody ready (after all, I was kind of the M.C. of the affair) and when they came in we all screamed, "Happy birthday!"

Never have I seen a person so flabbergasted, so stunned, so shaken. Her mouth fell open. Her legs seemed to buckle a bit. Her friend grabbed her arm to steady her. As she was led to sit on one of the stools along the counter, we all sang "Happy Birthday." As we came to the end of our singing . . . her eyes moistened. Then, when the birthday cake with all the candles on it was carried out, she lost it and just openly cried.

Harry gruffly mumbled, "Blow out the candles, Agnes! Come on! Blow out the candles! If you don't blow out the candles, I'm gonna hafta blow out the candles." And, after an endless few seconds, he did. Then he handed her a knife and told her, "Cut the cake, Agnes. Agnes, we all want some cake!"

Agnes looked down at the cake. Then without taking her eyes off it, she slowly and softly said, "Look, Harry, is it all right with you if I, I mean is it okay if I kind of, what I want to ask you is, is it O.K. if I keep the cake a little while? I mean, is it all right if we don't eat it right away?"

Harry shrugged and answered, "Sure! It's O.K. If you want to keep the cake, keep the cake. Take it home, if you want to."

"Can I?" she asked. Then, looking at me, she said, "I live just down the street a couple of doors. I want to take the cake home, okay? I'll be right back. Honest!" She got off the stool, picked up the cake, and carrying it like it was the Holy Grail, walked slowly toward the door. As we all just stood there motionless, she left.

When the door closed, there was a stunned silence in the place. Not knowing what else to do, I broke the silence by saying, "What do you say we pray?"

Looking back on it now, it seems more than strange for a sociologist to be leading a prayer meeting with a bunch of prostitutes in a diner in Honolulu at 3:30 in the morning. But then it just felt like the right thing to do. I prayed for Agnes. I prayed for her salvation. I prayed that her life would be changed and that God would be good to her.

When I finished, Harry leaned over the counter and with a trace of hostility in his voice, he said, "Hey! You never told me you were a preacher. What kind of church do you belong to?"

In one of those moments when just the right words came, I answered, "I belong to a church that throws birthday parties for whores at 3:30 in the morning."

Harry waited a moment and then almost sneered as he answered, "No you don't. There's no church like that. If there was, I'd join it. I'd join a church like that!"

Wouldn't we all? Wouldn't we all love to join a church that throws birthday parties for whores at 3:30 in the morning? Well, that's the kind of church that Jesus came to create! I don't know where we got the other one that's so prim and proper.[2]

It was reported that a congregation in a small country town in Australia took an innovative step toward reaching its community. A Melbourne newspaper announced, "Patrons of the Hamilton Hotel will soon be offered spirit of a different kind. In an unusual conversion, the town's Baptist Congregation—who are all teetotalers—have taken over one of the six pubs."

The Hamilton community watched in amazement as the pub, located on the main street opposite the local post office, was bought by the Baptists and renovated into a church and conference center. The front of the building was turned into a recreation area for young people, and its dance floor was converted into a chapel and a meeting room. The bar was transformed into a coffee shop, and the old pub became an alcohol-free building.

In the article, various church leaders from Melbourne and the pastor of the Hamilton Baptist Church spoke of the relocation as innovative, creative, and daring. However, one sour note sounded. Midway through the newspaper article, a local from Hamilton is quoted. One of the hotel's former regulars, an old farmer named Bruce McKellar, said he would miss his corner of the bar.

"I would walk in and straight to it; we all had our own space," he said. Farmer McKellar has been displaced from his personal seat at the bar, and he will never again be welcomed at his favorite watering hole.

In Australia, as in England, the local pub is a place of acceptance and friendship. Patrons develop allegiances to their pubs, and though they might visit another one occasionally, they feel a deep connection to their own pubs. American bars are not dissimilar, as we all want a place "where everybody knows our name." The farmers, factory workers, tradesmen, and business people of Hamilton, however, were shooed out of the Hamilton Hotel to make way for the clean and decent Baptists.

On the other side of the world, in the English town of Bradford, another group of Christians acquired another pub. The Cock & Bottle is a yellow, two-story English pub in a fierce, working-class town that is often violent and tormented by racial and class conflict. In the heart of this rough-and-tumble town is the "Bradford Christian Pub Consortium," which leases the Cock & Bottle. Malcolm Willis is the manager. Malcolm wants his pub to be a place of sanctuary and comfort, a place to call home, even a place of worship.

He and his wife live upstairs above the bar and take seriously the words of Jesus to "go into all the world" and "compel those" who have difficulty believing this great good news of grace to come to the party of God. They believe this going and compelling includes pubs. Willis says, "[Jesus] didn't say 'Sit in your church and wait for people to come to you.'"

The Willises and their staff, who are all Christians, have set about creating a loving, welcoming environment where locals are cared for, listened to, and ministered to. Says Willis, "Initially, many won't accept you talking about Jesus. Maybe after you've listened to them ten or twenty times—which can be exhausting—they might say 'Can you pray for me?' And then you see things happen."

These are not quick fixes. This is missional ministry over the long haul. Willis adds, "Yes, we're selling booze to people who could do without it. At least if they're here, we can get alongside them. Someone once showed me Proverbs 31, which says, 'Beer and wine are for the dying or for those who have lost all hope. Let them drink and forget how poor and miserable they feel. But you must defend those who are helpless and have no hope.' So I have to ask, 'What would Jesus have done?' I think the Lord would have been right here in the pubs."[3]

Late on a warm spring night in 1991, a young Asian teenager was seen running naked down the streets of Milwaukee. A woman saw the man and called 911. Paramedics arrived and put a blanket around the confused young man while police began asking questions. A tall, thin blond man arrived, claiming to be the teen's partner. The blond man explained that his dazed, naked friend had simply had too much to drink.

Things appeared normal enough, but just to be on the safe side, the two officers went with the teen and the tall blond man to his apartment. The apartment was neat, and the blond man apologized that his lover caused a disturbance and promised it would not happen again. The officers, not wanting to get in the middle of a domestic argument, left the apartment.

Two months later, on July 22, 1991, two Milwaukee police officers were patrolling the area surrounding Marquette University. Around midnight, as the two officers sat in their car, they saw a short, wiry black man with a handcuff dangling from his wrist. Assuming that this man had escaped from another policeman, they asked him what he was doing. The man started to pour out a tale about this "weird dude" who put the cuffs on him in his apartment. The two policemen thought they ought to check it out, and proceeded to the Oxford Apartments at 924 North 25th Street, the same apartment complex Milwaukee officers had visited two months earlier.

The handsome young blond man met them at the door. Upon entering the apartment, one of the officers noticed shocking graphic photographs lying around. The officers quickly handcuffed the man. What the officers then discovered made the entire world shiver, for this was the apartment of one of the most prolific serial killers in United States history. The young man in handcuffs was Jeffrey Dahmer.

There were human skulls in the refrigerator and freezer, on kitchen shelves and in cooking pots. Other body parts were preserved in formaldehyde. Some of the more gruesome Polaroid photos ever taken were locked in a bedroom closet. Jeffrey Dahmer had killed, mutilated, tortured, and cannibalized seventeen men and boys over a period of thirteen years. With his crimes so highly publicized, Dahmer was dead just three years after his arrest on that July night, beaten to death in prison by a fellow inmate.

When Dahmer faced the judge at the end of his trial, he said, "Your Honor, it is now over. This has never been a case of trying to get free. I didn't ever want freedom. Frankly, I wanted death for myself. I know how much harm I have caused. Thank God there will be no more harm that I can do." And then he added this: "I believe that only the Lord Jesus Christ can save me from my sins."[4]

Roy Ratcliff, a Church of Christ minister, arrived at the Columbia Correctional Institute on May 12, 1994, and based upon Dahmer's profession of faith in Jesus Christ as his Savior, Ratcliff baptized the murderer in the prison's whirlpool.[5]

Did Dahmer die a Christian? Did he lurch his way into the party of God? It is one thing for sinners of the garden variety to make it in the narrow door—sinners that look a little more like us. We can live with that. But this? A mass murderer? A deviant? As many skeptics have countered to Jeffrey Dahmer getting religion, "If Dahmer is going to be in heaven, then I don't want to go there. That is not the kind of heaven I want."

At the Great Banquet of God, when Christ will draw in all who belong to him, those who arrive as the guests of honor will not need your or my approval to get in the door. They will only need God's grace that throws the door open to all who will come. It could be that those who respond to that grace will not be the people we expect. If we were not already fully redeemed and in the presence of God, the kinds of people we will find there in our first moments inside the gates of heaven might be so shocking that the sight of them would otherwise kill us.

I do not know if Jeffrey Dahmer was a genuine follower of Christ or if he just got a convenient dose of jailhouse religion. I know as much about his heart as I know about anyone else's—not much. But I do know this: the grace that saves us from our "normal" sins, whatever "normal" may be, is the same grace that can save serial killers, potential suicide bombers, child molesters, rapists, and murderers.

For if God cannot save people like that, then God cannot save you or me. If God cannot save people like that, God cannot save anybody.

Notes

1. Stephanie Strom, "Wedding Off, Jilted Bride Turns Party Into a Benefit," *New York Times*, 8 September 2006.

2. Tony Campolo, *Let Me Tell You a Story* (Nashville: Word Publishing, 2000), 216–20.

3. The account of the "two bars" was first told and adapted from Michael Frost and Alan Hirsch, *The Shaping of Things to Come* (Peabody MA: Hendrickson Publishers, 2003), 9–11.

4. As quoted by the Associated Press for the *Milwaukee Journal*, 18 February 1992.

5. Steven Walters, "Dahmer Is Baptized in Prison Tub," *The Milwaukee Sentinel*, 12 May 1994. For Ratcliffe's complete account of his relationship with Dahmer, see his book *Dark Journey, Deep Grace* (Abiline: Leafwood, 2006).

Reflection Questions

1. I say "God's gracious salvation is nothing short of an outrageous scandal." Do you agree? Why or why not?

2. What do you think of Kyle Paxman's decision to transform her former wedding reception into a fundraiser for the poor?

3. Did Jesus come to create a church that, according to Tony Campolo, "throws birthday parties for whores at 3:30 in the morning"? Explain.

4. Do you think a group of Christians owning and operating a pub is an act of ministry or an act of compromise? Why or why not?

5. Do you think God saves those who commit what we consider the gravest sins, such as serial killers?

____

____

____

____

____

Chapter 9

Leaving Salem

"Jesus is Lord" is a radical claim, one that is ultimately rooted in questions of allegiance and ultimate authority.

—Lee Camp

Some time back I had my first experience with acupuncture. I felt like I was being placed into the care of a witch doctor, what with her barbs, magnets, electrodes, and stinky menthol oil. She might even have had a chicken foot or two in her bag. Still, my head was killing me and I needed relief, so I found myself lying down with needles in my hands, cheeks, forehead, and scalp. And then the electric shock therapy began.

My practitioner would find hotspots, points where "my pain was centered," she said, and there she would apply an electric probe. It worked. It actually relieved my migraine headache without causing any additional pain. But her techniques did alarm me at first, for when the probe was touched to a particular spot at the base of my skull, the needles in the top of my right hand would stand at attention and quiver. Such is the nerve connection of the human body.

Roger Williams—along with his beliefs and experiences—is like a lightning strike in the distant past. He has been dead for 300 years, and still the needles stand on end and dance, because of the current he continues to stir. He is still connected to the nerve center of many of us, so that when our lips move, our pens write, and our voices speak, it is Roger Williams we hear.

Roger Williams was born in London, England, in winter 1603. As a young man, he clerked for Sir Edward Coke, a brilliant attorney of his day and a man who once served as the chief justice of the British Empire. Coke took Williams in as his personal secretary and underwrote Williams's primary and secondary education, and in 1629, Williams was ordained in the Anglican Church.

Now, these were strange and dangerous days in England. Not everyone was happy with the Church of England. In fact, while Williams was pursuing his education and ordination, you might recall that a group of Separatists rebels left England in a little boat called the *Mayflower.* They landed at Plymouth Rock in a territory that would become known as the Massachusetts Bay Colony. These Pilgrims, in their simple black and white outfits and muzzle-loader rifles, left the comforts of home for religious freedom. They had been oppressed and persecuted by the state church and had set out for the New World to create a type of religious utopia. The Pilgrims were not very successful, and a decade later, under a new charter, they were replaced by the Puritans. John Winthrop, the first governor of the newly chartered colony, explained that the Puritans intended to create a "city on a hill," so the nations of the world might see how God's people were to live.

Roger Williams was irresistibly drawn to this kind of inspirational idealism. In 1630, he and his wife set sail for Massachusetts and the promise of freedom from religious coercion. In the New World, Williams became pastor of the small Puritan congregation that gathered in Salem, Massachusetts, and it did not take him long to get into trouble. At Salem Roger Williams began sharing his religious ideas from the pulpit, but not all his parishioners were receptive.

What was it about Roger Williams's preaching that caused him so much trouble? He believed that the state had no right to enforce religion, and he believed in the odd idea that there should be a separation between church and state. Further, he felt individuals should pursue a relationship with God as dictated by their understanding of God, without outside interference. Expressing such ideas was like dropping an atomic bomb.

Massachusetts had thrown off the oppression of the Church of England but had replaced it with an oppression of its own making. The persecuted, as often happens, became the persecutors. The Puritans condemned the Anglicans for burning their own at the stake, but turned around and did the same to others. They developed a complex system of religious rules and regulations that everyone in the colony was expected to follow, even if following the regulations meant violating one's conscience. Ministers in the churches became spies, looking over people's shoulders, keeping them in line. If you failed to show up on Sunday at church, the police might appear at your door Monday morning to put you in jail. If you didn't tithe on your income, the governor of the state could increase your taxes. The minister got his paycheck from the municipality's coffers, and the collection on Sunday was sent to city hall. If you were running for office, you had better get the endorsement of the local minister, for only those he deemed godly could be elected.

And when it came to voting, only those who were members of the church were allowed to vote.

Roger Williams stood in the pulpit at Salem, Massachusetts, and courageously refused to yield to such practices and beliefs, preaching a freedom from and within religion. Consequently, on September 13, 1635, the Massachusetts General Court convicted Roger Williams of "new and dangerous opinions" and banished him from the Province. When he continued to preach, protected largely by his integrity and a very vigorous following, the authorities made plans to kidnap him and deport him to England as an enemy of the crown. He was tipped off just hours before the authorities arrived with the blunt words of a friend, "Get thee gone from Salem and do not return."

In winter 1636, Roger placed his wife and newborn daughter in the protective hands of his friends and left Salem in the middle of the night. He spent the next weeks trying to survive the New England wilderness and winter, often near starvation. Native Americans of the region befriended him and kept him alive, and he eventually purchased from the Narragansett tribe land that would become the state of Rhode Island. Rhode Island became a haven for all kinds of dissidents in the earliest years of the American colonies. The first American Quakers, Jews, Anabaptists, and Baptists came to Rhode Island to escape the religious persecution of the Puritans and others; while Roger did not agree with the beliefs of all these groups, he still believed that these people had the right to choose and express their faith according to their own consciences—and not according to the rules of a church or a government.

Williams went on to organize the first Baptist church on American soil, in Providence, but eventually left it as well to become only a "Seeker" after Christ. At great personal cost to his reputation, his finances, his family, and comfort, Roger Williams sought only to follow Jesus, and he invited others to do the same.[1]

Sometimes the appeal from our church pulpits should look more like a lonely Roger Williams stumbling through the snow than the massive, smiling, therapeutic gatherings of Christians who have a hard time hearing and heeding the startling words, "When Christ calls a man, he bids him come and die."[2] Yet that is exactly what Jesus demands:

Come and die.

Take up your cross.

Join the journey from which there is no return.

This is an open, gracious invitation to radical freedom—but it is not always easy.

> A large crowd was following Jesus. He turned around and said to them, "If you want to be my disciple, you must hate everyone else by comparison—your father and mother, wife and children, brothers and sisters—yes, even your own life. Otherwise, you cannot be my disciple. And if you do not carry your own cross and follow me, you cannot be my disciple.
>
> "But don't begin until you count the cost. For who would begin construction of a building without first calculating the cost to see if there is enough money to finish it? Otherwise, you might complete only the foundation before running out of money, and then everyone would laugh at you. They would say, 'There's the person who started that building and couldn't afford to finish it!'
>
> "Or what king would go to war against another king without first sitting down with his counselors to discuss whether his army of 10,000 could defeat the 20,000 soldiers marching against him? And if he can't, he will send a delegation to discuss terms of peace while the enemy is still far away. So you cannot become my disciple without giving up everything you own. (Luke 14:25-33)

The procession to Jerusalem has been joined by many would-be followers of Jesus. Huge crowds press in upon him. The original twelve disciples are now outnumbered a hundred to one. Those who have been harmed and marginalized by the religionists, those who suffer at the lower rungs of society or the economy, those who long for freedom from Rome's oppression see in Jesus their revolutionary moment. They will hitch their wagon to his star and follow him into the glory of kingdom-come. Jesus does not encourage this mob to follow him another step. Instead, he stops to rebuke them.

He warns them not to take on a project that they could not ultimately afford, like a costly construction project or the declaration of war, which once begun must be completed.

"Following me is no easy thing," he is saying. "Don't pursue me out of impulsive emotion or what you think you will get. Take the time to deliberate. Think about it."

In the spirit of informed consent and full disclosure, Jesus wanted any who would follow him to know exactly what they were getting into. This was a pricey enterprise exceeding that of buildings and kingdoms. To follow Jesus meant relinquishing all competing agendas: family, religion, nationalism, economics, politics—the people were told to leave all of these alongside the Jerusalem road. There was no other way.

I find this to be one of the more challenging episodes in Jesus' ministry. Should not the ambition of a "good" pastor and the sign of a "successful" church be a large bustling crowd? Getting as many voices behind the Jesus-mob, is that not that the idea? Rear-ends in the pews, dollars in the plate, names on the roll, baptisms on the annual report; that is the name of the game, right?

Apparently not.

The one who said "Come unto me" is now intentionally running people away. Yet, if he had not done so, he would not have been a very honest Messiah, for the path of Christ leads to a cross, not a chicken in every pot and an SUV in every garage. The people clambering after him on this day failed to understand that. Who Jesus actually was and who they wanted him to be were two different things.

Granted, these followers on the Jerusalem road were not the only ones with this problem. For millennia we have looked at this man Jesus and shaped him according to our wishes. Search the images of "Jesus" on the Internet and you will find all sorts of representations from the iconic to the perverted. You will find Jesus wrapped in an American flag, Jesus with his head thrown back in laughter, Jesus Christ Superstar, Jesus on a Harley Davidson, Jesus as a CEO, Jesus the homosexual, Jesus of all different nationalities and races, Jesus as your "homeboy," even a Jesus with boxing gloves ready to take on all challengers.

In my own life I have known several Jesuses. It is likely that you have too. As a child and teenager I met the "save me from hell Jesus." That was all he was really good for: to keep me from burning in the afterlife. Later, in Bible College and in studying theology I drew close to the "advocate Jesus," the one who stood between me and an angry God in the cosmic courtroom. He was the one who judicially took my place and passed his goodness on to me. As a pastor and social justice activist, out in the rough and tumble world away from the academy, you find that people have marriage problems, are diagnosed with cancer, live in poverty, suffer from mental illness, and have to bury their children. There I met the "incarnate Jesus" who identifies with the poor, the downtrodden, and the suffering. He is the one present in the least of these.

I later discovered the "example Jesus" who is more than a way to get to heaven and avoid hell. His life and teachings are a template for how we should live today. And of course I love the "rebel Jesus," who has raised his head often in the pages of this book, the Jesus who threw off all religious conformity. I have known all these Jesuses, and probably a few more I am ashamed to admit. Which one is the right one? Which one is real? Jesus might be the same yesterday, today, and forever, but how do we weed through all these images to get to the authentic Son of God?

Reverend Ken Autry is the former pastor at First United Methodist Church in Defuniak Springs, Florida. I say "former" pastor only because he has now moved on to another appointment. Those Methodists will not let their preachers sit still for very long. I was once listening to one of his sermons when he shared a letter with his congregation that I have yet to get out of my mind. The letter had been written by a parishioner who had become quite disgruntled with her pastor.

I would like to say that disgruntled congregants are uncommon. They are not. Sometimes there is the perception that those of the cloth should be absolutely faultless. When failures occur, and they certainly will, the fallout can be devastating. Sure, there are some bad apples in the barrel, but most pastors, priests, and rabbis are doing the best they can to honor their calling and to help others. They make mistakes. We all do.

This particular church member gave no quarter for such ministerial blunders. With her teeth on edge she poured out a venomous letter to the pastor. She recounted his failures. She demeaned his family. She compared him to other great pastors that had gone before him (always good for one's self-esteem), and pretty much read him the riot act. It was the conclusion of the letter that still rings in my ears.

She wrote, "I pray that you will come to know Jesus as *I* do, rather than just knowing Jesus like *you* do."

Such a statement, more revealing than insulting, is why religion almost always wins out over Jesus. When people start talking about their experience with Jesus, the religious establishment gets nervous. What if that Jesus – their Jesus – does not match our Jesus? So the variegated stripes and flavors of the Christian religion have come up with definitive answers to such questions. Rules have been set. Boundaries have been well defined. Security and safety measures have been implemented. Why? So no one strays off message, so no one believes in, follows, or experiences the wrong Jesus.

Many of our cherished doctrinal statements are not for the sake of communicating what we believe. They are for the purpose of protecting us and our adherents from a Christ that colors outside the lines of what we find acceptable.

Yes, I admit there is a danger in following only the Jesus of our personal experience. He can become nothing more than a Rorschach ink blot test. We see in him what we want to see. On the other hand, when Jesus is defined solely by controlled interpretations of the Bible, regardless of human experience, he is given no room to surprise us, to work in ways that do not fit our preconceptions. He is reduced to a little statue to carry around in our pocket, or a plastic bobble head doll on the dashboard of our car. It is idolatry.

It takes some courage to admit that any interpretation of Jesus is faulty, but such an admission is necessary. Why? Because all interpretations of Jesus must be translated through imperfect human beings and the sight-limiting culture in which we all live. Thus, our interpretations will be imperfect and fallible. To say these interpretations are otherwise is to fail to recognize that we are often like those Roman soldiers who carried out the scourging of Jesus. They conveniently dressed him in their own clothes, and only then did they bow down to worship him.[3]

The spirit of the Reformation must always be alive within the Christian community. We must remain in a state of pliable alteration, sensitive to the Spirit's leadership, because our conclusions about God, Jesus, the Bible, even our own spiritual experiences, are incomplete. They will never be settled in this lifetime. For we know Christ, but we do not know him. We press forward with confidence in our faith, and yet we learn to hold to our conclusions loosely. "Here we stand, we can do no other," and still we know our beliefs will change over the course of our lifetimes. "This is what we believe," and yet what we believe is in process.

The "real" Jesus is in our hearts. He is in the midst of his worshiping church. He meets us at the Communion table. He is revealed to us in the Scriptures. He is on the road to Jerusalem. He is found in life's troubles and victories. But when we speak of him we are speaking only of our understanding about him, for he remains elusively out of our reach. So the short answer is this: Yes, we know Jesus, but we do not *know* him, and we will not know him this side of the consummation of the kingdom of God. Even then the mystery of God's love in Christ will unravel for all eternity. The journey of following Christ will continue beyond this life.

Years ago my sister traveled to Eastern Europe, Russia, and the Ukraine on an extended mission trip. She worked among the indigenous Christians on a number of worthy projects, and when her time ran up, she returned home with a heart full of joy, a head full of memories, and bags full of strange and wonderful souvenirs. Since I am the only twin brother my sister has, she brought me a unique gift. I got a set of Babushka dolls, those traditional Russian nesting dolls. When the first doll is opened, it has a smaller doll on the inside, so on and so forth, until the end result is a tiny weeble-wobble deep within.

Actually my gift was not that special. You can pick up Babushkas for pennies on the rubles. When my sister thought of me she probably thought, "How little can I spend and still appear thoughtful?" Whatever. I know how it works.

Anyway, this was after Russian *Perestroika*, Polish *Solidarity*, and the other movements that unhinged communism in Eastern Europe. At the time Boris Yeltsin was president of what was left of the Soviet regime. So, the outer doll of my Babushka set was, entertainingly, Boris Yeltsin. His likeness had a dopey little smile and rumpled hair as if he had been drinking too much vodka (accurately portrayed, I fear). When Yeltsin was opened, there was Gorbachev with the familiar birthmark on his forehead. Inside Gorbachev was Khrushchev, then Josef Stalin, and finally Vladimir Lenin himself. I now keep all these little Communists boxed in the attic. They are much too dangerous to be let loose in the world again.

The deeper you explored these dolls, the closer you got to the essence of Soviet power, its source and beginning. As layer after layer fell away, and finally you held a tiny characterization of Lenin in your hand, you could truthfully say, "Ah, now I have gotten to the bottom of it all. This is the seed, the kernel from which all others grew."

I, and many others, have tried this with Jesus. We have struggled to unravel him, to break open his shell, and then the next, and the next, and the next. We think we can get to the bottom of who he is. We reconstruct his historical setting. We dissect his words. We set out to determine who he "really was" and is. But there is a problem. When dealing with this Jesus, we do not find ourselves moving to something smaller and more manageable. The deeper we go, as the layers fall away, we move to something greater. He gets larger, more uncontrollable, more inconceivable, more wonderfully unmanageable than our minds can imagine.

Yet, there is a seed, a core to the historical Jesus as well as the exalted Christ of our faith. It is the element of sacrifice. There at the end of it all, when the onion is peeled, is a cross—for him—and his followers. There is a cross hanging above my desk where these words are being typed. I wear a crucifix around my neck. I even have a Celtic version of the symbol inked into my skin. I behold the cross every day, yet cannot take hold of all its implications. Still, this cannot prevent me from taking hold of the cross for myself. In the words of John Howard Yoder: "To be a disciple is to share in that style of life of which the cross is the culmination."[4]

Jesus put it more bluntly: "If you do not carry your own cross and follow me, you cannot be my disciple."

In the immediate years following the birth of Jesus, there were no fewer than three major messianic movements in Palestine.[5] Men of the peasant class, not unlike Jesus, rallied to themselves bands of disciples and enthusiastic crowds. Many of these came right out of Jesus' home region of Galilee. Messianic hopes rippled across the countryside only to be crushed again and again by the world's superpower. Three legions of Roman soldiers poured into Galilee to squash these rebellions. The resulting slaughter was cataclysmic. The capital of Galilee was burned to the ground, its people put in chains, and the surrounding villages were ransacked. The Romans crucified on crosses two thousand followers of these prospective messiahs.

When Jesus turned to the crowds following him to Jerusalem and said, "If you do not carry your own cross and follow me, you cannot be my disciple," every thinking adult in the crowd would not have thought of a hypothetical or spiritualized possibility of self-sacrifice. They would have remembered the sites and smells of the skeletal corpses hanging along the highways and byways of Galilee. They would have remembered the clear and violent message of Rome tattooed on their brains since childhood: "This is what happens to revolutionaries. This is what we do to messiahs and their followers."

When Jesus introduced a cross into the equation he could not have made a more sobering, deflating statement. It would be like demanding today that someone gladly bear their electric chair to their own execution, or that they be gloriously fitted with a noose in advance of their own hanging. Jesus will only take those foolish enough to embrace death as the means to gaining life.

Yes, Jesus is declaring in advance his and his followers' demise. As he warned the band of twelve before beginning this journey he warns everyone within earshot: "This journey ends with a cross." Of course, Jesus would turn the cross into a symbol of triumph. He would take all the evil the world could throw at him and absorb it into his own flesh. He would defeat death with the rising sun of Easter Sunday, himself rising back to life. But such an outcome was impossible for this crowd of eager revolutionaries to anticipate.

January 13, 1982, was a cold, snowy day in the nation's capital. A massive blizzard delayed the travel of commuters trying to get home and air-travelers trying to leave the city. At the height of the storm, Air Florida Flight 90 took off from Washington D.C.'s National Airport. Just seconds in the air, its wings heavy with snow and ice, the plane struck the 14th Street Bridge and plunged into the icy waters of the Potomac River.

The attempted helicopter rescue of the precious few survivors was viewed on the nation's television sets all afternoon. Hundreds of onlookers gathered on the damaged bridge and the snow covered banks of the river to watch as well. One man was twenty-eight-year-old Lenny Skutnik, a gopher in the Congressional Budget office.

Lenny had a simple life with his wife and two young sons. He had never taken a life-saving or first aid course. Making less than $15,000 a year, paying the $325 a month rent was his biggest regular challenge. Yet, when he saw a woman, Priscilla Tirado, blinded by shock and jet fuel, too weak to grasp the rings being lowered by the rescue helicopter, Lenny quickly went from being an observer to a participant in a daring act of courage. He jumped into the freezing water after her, pulling her to shore and to safety.[6]

Later that month President Reagan seated Lenny Skutnik next to the First Lady as his special guest for the State of the Union address. Lenny was the first "ordinary" American to receive such an honor. President Reagan said, "Nothing had picked Lenny out particularly to be a hero, but without hesitation there he was and he saved her life."

Skutnik resisted all efforts to make his risky act into something extraordinary. He said, "Nobody else was doing anything. It was the only way . . . I just did it."[7]

Those who follow Christ are not fearless adrenaline junkies who possess super-spirituality, and who are immune to failure. Nothing could be further from the truth. They are simply those who, even in throat-strangling fear, say their prayers and jump into the water. Yes, the water is cold. Yes, the dangers are many. Yes, the risk is great. But they roll the dice and place their bets on Jesus anyway.

Saul of Tarsus was just such a betting man. You may remember that he was a religious walk-the-line, do-things-by-the-book, jump-through-all-the-right-hoops, make-God-proud kind of guy. A pure-blooded, pedigreed descendent of father Abraham and a practicing Pharisee, he was so committed to the true religion of God that he declared war on the movement surrounding the followers of Jesus. Saul viewed the movement as a dangerous heresy that had to be stamped out. He put his energies into doing just that. Saul was an enforcer, holding the people's feet to the religious fire, or at the very least threatening people with that fire.

But this highly motivated soldier of God, this religious zealot convinced beyond any discussion that he was right and everyone else was wrong, had his life dismantled in a single moment by Jesus. Acts 9 records Saul's much-celebrated conversion on the Damascus road. He was on his way to arrest and imprison Christians when Jesus met him on the road in blinding light, calling Saul to a new journey. Saul's hardness of heart was melted and he became the greatest Christian missionary the world has ever witnessed, the first to take the gospel to the European continent changing the course of the world.

In light of his experience with Jesus, what did Saul do with all of his spiritual accomplishments? Did he incorporate them into his newfound life with Christ? Did he hang on to all of it for emergency back-up should things not work out in his newly chosen path? No. He threw it all away.

These familiar words bear repeating: "I once thought these things were valuable, but now I consider them worthless because of what Christ has done. . . . For his sake I have discarded everything else, counting it all as garbage, so that I could gain Christ and become one with him" (Phil 3:7-9a).

Saul, now called Paul, goes into his office after his conversion. He sits down in his high-back leather chair behind his oak desk and begins to review his religious career. In a moment he is on his feet. He rips his diplomas off the wall and the frames shatter on the floor. The prized picture of him shaking the high priest's hand? He chunks it in the garbage can. The letter of commendation from the Jerusalem Temple for his commitment to missions and theological orthodoxy? He wads it in a ball and zings across the room. The honorary doctorate from the Jewish academy at Tiberius? He burns it in the wastebasket. He throws his family's crest and coat of arms, traced thousands of years all the way back to Abraham, out the window. Why? He considers it all garbage for the sake of knowing and gaining Christ. That is the trade—the gamble—he made.

The word he uses for "garbage" in the New Living Translation gets various treatments depending upon the English translation. The New International Version and New American Standard Bible use the word "rubbish." The New Century Version calls Paul's former life "worthless trash."

But the King James Version and Eugene Peterson's *The Message* pull no punches: They both call it "dung."

The Greek word is *skubalon,* and yes, it means dung. Manure. Compost. Crap. The well-educated, prim and proper, golden-tongued Apostle Paul has reached into the dictionary of slang and four-letter words for this description. It is *skubalon.*

Paul came to the realization that his extensive religion and all his religious activity, as big as it was, was inadequate. He learned that his God was too small. This Christ, who revealed who God really was, was so consuming there was no room for anything else. All that Paul held onto, when compared to Christ, was junk.

For those who call themselves disciples, nothing matters but following this same Jesus. Not our denomination, not our Catholicism, Protestantism or religious label, not our preferred doctrinal system, not our favored biblical interpretations, not our religious upbringing, our training or heritage, our high steeples or stained glass. None of these are worthy of our allegiance. None of these are worthy of our worship. These are lesser things that if we hold to them as primary, will prevent us from pursing Christ, who called all other allegiances "hate" in comparison to the allegiance he demands.

Even our nationality, our democratic way of life, our economic policies, and our political parties do not deserve our ultimate and final allegiance. As followers of Jesus, we reserve that right exclusively for him. This is a surprise for some, but true nonetheless: Jesus is not a white, middle-class Republican. Jesus is not a Democrat, a Libertarian, a Marxist, or a Socialist. Jesus is not a Baptist, a Catholic, a Lutheran, or a Buddhist. Jesus isn't even a Christian. Jesus Christ is Lord.

Followers of Jesus are not those who vote a certain way, who answer exit polls in a predefined bloc, who are born in a specific country, or those who line up the correct way on two or three hot-button political issues. Followers of Jesus are those who have thrown themselves on Christ alone, letting go of everything else, scorning the consequences.[8]

When the church gathers to worship and to do missions, it is gathering and going as the distinct people of God, a people without regard to race, socio-economic status, gender, or the other lesser allegiances that separate people. These were all obliterated at the cross of Christ and in the cross-bearing lifestyle he demands. The glue that holds the church together is not the place of our birth, the Revolutionary War of the past or the War on Terror of the present. It is not the Declaration of Independence, the Constitution, rulings from the Supreme Court, or any other musty document stored in the basement of the Smithsonian. We are not held together by family bloodlines, by *ex cathedra* statements from the Vatican, the writings of the Reformers, or the preaching of today's leading evangelicals.

The bond that unites all believers is the person of Jesus Christ, who has called us to our own death. Our allegiance is to him. He is our King. He is our Lord. It is his kingdom we supremely serve. All other kingdoms and empires—whether they are nations, economies, families, respectability, popularity, security, denominations, or our systemized explanations of everything divine—these are all secondary allegiances. Only Christ is worthy of the call to bear a cross and follow his example.

The late devotional writer and Catholic priest Henri Nouwen compared the leap of faith we must make to follow Christ to the courage of a trapeze artist. This was something Nouwen knew about first hand. Nouwen traveled with the "Flying Rodleighs" for a time, drawing more than one spiritual lesson from the lives they lived. He said, like a high-flying trapeze artist, we must let go of the security we have had, to take hold of what is coming to us. And like a trapeze artist, we cannot do both at the same time.

Follow this line of thought. In the moment that a trapeze artist moves from one trapeze bar to the next, she must leave the relative security of holding on to something solid, something that has her confidence, and keeps her from falling. Then she must stretch out for the bar that is coming to her. In those milliseconds, which probably seem like an eternity, she is hanging there in mid-air—with nothing—her life at stake. She can neither go back to the security she has known, nor speed the next trapeze bar to her. It is an act of faith.

The life of following and knowing Christ is lived in those moments between the trapeze bars. We cannot go back to our former lives, the way we used to believe, think, and live. We let those things go in order to follow Christ. Yet, we have not taken hold of all that we hope for. With sweaty palms and racing hearts, our very lives nailed to a cross, we have given our supreme allegiance to Christ and an adventurous though unknown future.

A final ironic and tragic note: With this kind of cross-bearing, adventurous courage, Roger Williams created a shelter for those seeking religious freedom. There was a lot of diversity, a lot of disagreement, a lot of impassioned attempts at conversion, but the commitment was there to let people be. Roger Williams became a name associated with freedom, toleration, and liberty.

Do you remember what happened back at Salem?

In summer 1692, five years after the death of Roger Williams, the religious hysteria machine ran roughshod over the Massachusetts colony and much of New England. The infamous witch hunt that took scores of lives, harmed hundreds if not thousands, and placed the blackest of marks on our collective history, all began in that little church and community where Roger Williams once preached.

It will sometimes cost us a great deal to follow Christ and conscience. But it may cost us far more to stay where we are.

Notes

1. Edwin S. Gaustad is a leading authority on the life of Roger Williams. See his books *Liberty of Conscience* (Valley Forge: Judson Press, 1999) and *Roger Williams* (New York: Oxford Press, 2005).

2. Dietrich Bonhoeffer, *The Cost of Discipleship*, rev. ed. (New York: Macmillan, 1963), 99.

3. This phrasing was inspired by Stephen Prothero, *American Jesus; How the Son of God Became a National Icon* (New York: Farrar, Straus and Giroux, 2003), 297.

4. John Howard Yoder, *The Politics of Jesus* (Grand Rapids: Eerdmans, 1994), 38.

5. John Dominic Crossan, *The Historical Jesus* (New York: HarperCollins, 1992), 198–204.

6. William J. Bennett, *The Book of Virtues* (New York: Simon and Schuster, 1993), 505–507.

7. See Ronald Reagan, "Address Before a Joint Session of the Congress Reporting on the State of the Union, January 26, 1982," The American Presidency Project, http://www.presidency.ucsb.edu/ws/index.php?pid=42687; and James R. Hood, "Strangers to the Rescue," ConsumerAffairs.com, 18 December 2006, http://www.consumeraffairs.com/news04/2006/12/transplant_strangers.html.

8. Clarence Jordan often defined faith as living "a life in scorn of the consequences." I am indebted to him for this expression.

Reflection Questions

1. How have we been guilty of presenting the gospel as a self-improvement plan rather than a sacrificial way of life? Why do we seem to make the gospel less demanding than it is?

2. Can we reconcile the demands of Jesus found in this chapter with our desire for larger churches and bigger crowds? If so, how?

3. I mention the different Jesuses I have known. What Jesuses have you known in your time as a Christian?

4. Are our doctrinal statements declarations of what we believe or protection from those we do not want to let in? Explain.

5. Crucifixion was not a hypothetical possibility for those who first followed Jesus. What would this level of sacrifice look like for us today?

____

____

____

____

____

Chapter 10

God Ain't a Quitter

> It is hard to escape the conclusion that today one of the greatest roadblocks to the Gospel of Jesus Christ is the institutional church.
>
> —Howard A. Snyder

Aussie Peter Chapman maintains a fun website that ranks Bible verses by frequency of use. He started with a program that counted and ranked biblical references on the Internet. Now he uses a nifty little search engine called www.topverses.com. No, this is not a paid advertisement.

A visit to that site revealed how wrong I was. See, I thought for sure that Luke 15, with its trio of "lost" parables (a lost sheep, a lost coin, and a lost son) would be near the top in Bible-reading popularity. Not even close. What is the most referenced Bible verse in cyberspace? No surprises here: John 3:16. In fact, good old John has the top three (John 1:1 and John 14:6, numbers 2 and 3 respectively).

Matthew and Genesis get in on the action once each, and pretty much everything else in the top ten belongs to the Apostle Paul. Luke does not even get a shout out until seventy-sixth place. And Luke 15? It finally gets a reference at the 204th mark. At least it did not come in last. That distinction belongs to some obscure genealogy in Chronicles.[1]

Maybe it is personal disappointment over the rankings, but I have given a lot of thought to why Luke 15 is not more popular. I think it is because this triplet of stories reveals a God that makes most Bible readers and Bible thumpers uncomfortable. These stories say things about God and his grace that we prefer to ignore. While we love the graciousness found in these stories, we love for that grace to fall on us, not necessarily on those outside our circle.

The third story, the Parable of the Prodigal Son as it is commonly called, will get its own chapter in the pages ahead. Here, we begin with that story's two younger siblings; stories that serve as partners and a prelude to Jesus' revealing of a scandalous God.

> Tax collectors and other notorious sinners often came to listen to Jesus teach. This made the Pharisees and teachers of religious law complain that he was associating with such sinful people—even eating with them!
>
> So Jesus told them this story: "If a man has a hundred sheep and one of them gets lost, what will he do? Won't he leave the ninety-nine others in the wilderness and go to search for the one that is lost until he finds it? And when he has found it, he will joyfully carry it home on his shoulders. When he arrives, he will call together his friends and neighbors, saying, 'Rejoice with me because I have found my lost sheep.' In the same way, there is more joy in heaven over one lost sinner who repents and returns to God than over ninety-nine others who are righteous and haven't strayed away!
>
> "Or suppose a woman has ten silver coins and loses one. Won't she light a lamp and sweep the entire house and search carefully until she finds it? And when she finds it, she will call in her friends and neighbors and say, 'Rejoice with me because I have found my lost coin.' In the same way, there is joy in the presence of God's angels when even one sinner repents." (Luke 15:1-10)

There was a time when Jesus could be found eating with the religious leaders of his day. No longer. They quit inviting him to their cocktail parties when he refused to conform to their standards of doctrine and conduct. What else could they do? Sharing a table with someone in Jewish society was not unlike the social dynamic of our own day. You eat with those you like, with those of whom you approve, with those you consider friends, if not family. The oft-quoted invitation in our churches, "come join the food, fun, and fellowship," is completely accurate. Mealtime is where more than bread is broken; barriers are broken as well. We share food, conversation, time, and life together. This is an act of communion reserved for those with whom we enjoy some kind of meaningful relationship.

Thus we see the problem: Jesus was socializing and eating with "tax collectors and other notorious sinners" (v. 1). It seems that when the Pharisees took Jesus off their invite list, he found another group with which to associate, for he goes where he is welcome. But this group, at least in the eyes of the robe-clad clergy, was not worthy of friendship—not even for a self-styled rabbi like Jesus.

Who were these "notorious sinners"? Who knows for sure? They were likely a collection of social outcasts and the ones your mother warned you to stay away from. Barflies, prostitutes, addicts, drunks, gang members, the sexually questionable, the indicted and paroled: you get the idea. This was a salty crowd.

"Sinners" by Pharisaic standards were outsiders to the ways of the one true God. They were those who by nationality or behavior had alienated themselves from the temple and the law. Luke should know, for he was just such an outsider. He was a Gentile.

Gerhard Lenski has written extensively about the class divisions found within ancient societies.[2] The division, simplifying his taxonomy, is twofold. The upper class consisted of those who ruled and governed, the merchants, and the priestly class. Across a gulf impossible to span was the lower class. These were peasants and farmers, artisans and laborers, the unclean and the "expendable"—the criminals, beggars, and outlaws. While Jesus was keeping company with those he found welcoming, following Lenski's rationale, Luke 15 finds Jesus surrounded by the lower class of Jewish society, in friendship even with the unclean and expendable.

This is confirmed when we note that "tax collectors" were in this crowd. Tax collectors, certainly expendable by many evaluations, were more than helpful representatives of the Internal Revenue Service. Tax collectors were employed by the Roman government to collect tribute from the empire's occupied territories. The Romans would auction off a territory to the highest bidder. The winning bid would then serve as the tax due from the territory in question. So when the winning bidder went to collect taxes, he was not actually collecting for the Romans; he was collecting for himself to recover and improve upon his investment.

In a largely agrarian, uneducated society, few knew what their actual tax bill was and had little recourse to correct injustices. So tax collecting was rife with obscene levels of over-taxation and extortion. As a consequence, tax collectors were hated for not only collaborating with and giving comfort to the enemy, but also for being obvious criminals breaking the backs of the populace while enjoying the protection of foreign invaders. They were truly expendable.

Jesus is not an uncouth, bad-mannered hillbilly from Galilee who failed to understand the social and religious significance of those with whom he shared a meal. He understood it quite well, for he sat with these outcasts intentionally. It was not for the sake of making the religious establishment angry, though he knew they would be angry. It was to show that God had come to the world not with a fuming, clinched fist, but with a compassionate, open hand.

The stage for Luke 15 is then set, with the unclean and expendable classes happily enjoying supper with Jesus the "friend of sinners" on one hand, juxtaposed against the seething, grumbling Pharisees and teachers of the religious law on the other.

Not long ago, while tooling through the Deep South, I saw an amazing sight. In a small town, tucked away between rolling hills and cotton fields, was a religious compound. At least that's what I think it was. The "Landmark Baptist Encampment" had obviously acquired the facilities of a long-discarded school. There they had set up a refuge of sorts, an "encampment." It was not a "camp," not a "campground," not a "retreat." It was an encampment. That got my attention.

The place lived up to its name. A high chain-link fence surrounded the building and grounds. The driveway was gated. Rolls of barbed wire wrapped around the top of the fence. Large "No Trespassing" signs glared at passersby. It looked like a detention facility. Maybe it was. I don't know. Several sad-looking children sat out front in the summer heat. They had the look of those who wished they were somewhere else—anywhere else—but there.

Now, the Landmark Baptist Encampment may be a wonderful place to camp, go fishing, ride horses, or do whatever happy campers want to do. It may be led by some of the most compassionate and kind people in the world. I'm merely saying it sure didn't look like it. As the encampment wilted away in my rearview mirror, I couldn't help thinking that it was a sadly accurate representation of so much of the church.

Fences.

Walls.

Gated doors.

"No Trespassing" signs.

Keep out.

As a Christian, I believe that Jesus is the Son of God. Without question I firmly accept him as the true and living way, the unique Word and revelation of God. When I read the Gospels, particularly stretches like this Great Journey to Jerusalem, I find that Jesus was also one of the most welcoming personalities the world has ever received. Did this mean Jesus threw his arms around every yahoo who came along and with a casual wave of his hand said it didn't matter how a person lived his or her life? Of course not. Sin and wayward decisions have disastrous consequences. But let it not be missed that the accusation the religious community always brought against Jesus was this: "He is a friend to sinners."

Could such an accusation be laid at the feet of the church today? Would such an indictment stick? "See those people over there? They love and befriend sinners."

I wonder.

Sadly, you do not have to travel to an obscure campground to see religious "Keep Out" signs. The establishment is good at sorting the sheep from the goats and the wheat from the weeds.

This one is in. That one is out.

This one passes. That one fails.

This one is approved. That one is rejected.

Through careful examination and inspection, only those with acceptable morals, beliefs, and lifestyles, those who have signed off on all the correct doctrinal statements of orthodoxy, are allowed in the door. This morality policing is done with God's blessing, of course. For God is on our team. He is inside our fence. He authorized our "Keep Out" signs. Thus, to argue with the rules or their enforcement is to oppose God himself. So goes the threadbare argument.

We can build fences, string concertina wire, and lock the gates to keep out everything and everyone we find polluted, fearful, and threatening. In the end, we may succeed in this task. But what will we gain if the world outside perishes, while we remain safe, comfortable, and pure? I don't know what is gained, but I know what is lost: Christ himself. For Jesus was found "out there" in the contamination from which the religious community always tries to distance itself.

Yes, there are those who say wall-destroying behavior is too risky, too compromising, too far out of bounds, but tearing down our religious fences simply means our love for others is stronger than our insecurities, our fears, and our ravenous need to be right. Being a "friend of sinners" is an accusation that Christians should wear as a badge of honor, for nothing could honor Jesus more, and nothing is more revealing of who God actually is.

Just look at these two parables Jesus tells.

The first parable involves shepherding, a common occupation in Jesus' day, and a familiar concept ascribed to God. The prophets often compared God's people to sheep, with him as their shepherd (see Isa 40 and 53;

Ezek 34; and Mic 5). The psalmists echo this theme, particularly Psalm 23, written by the shepherd king himself, David. The jump from the pasture to the synagogue was an easy one for Jesus. Quite effortlessly, God is introduced as the seeking shepherd of a poor lost sheep.

A shepherd led his sheep out of the pen early each morning to graze on the surrounding hillsides. Like golf balls scattered across the practice range, the sheep spread out over the terrain, far and wide, but always remained under the watchful eye of the shepherd. In the evening, with full bellies, the sheep were led home to the pen. There the shepherd counted them as they entered the gate. Often it was late in the day when he discovered a sheep was missing. The shepherd had a choice: leave the lost sheep out in the wild for the night, exposed to all manner of danger, and be grateful for ninety-nine in the pen, or leave immediately to find the lost animal.

Jesus paints the picture of a shepherd who realizes a sheep is missing while the entire herd is still out grazing. This shepherd will not wait until the evening to begin his search. He is afraid to leave the animal in distress any longer than necessary, so he leaves the remainder of his sheep behind (shepherding was a communal task; he would have left them in the care of others) and begins immediately searching for the lost one. Ninety-nine bawling, hungry sheep are surely enough to keep the shepherd busy, but one lost sheep is one too many. The shepherd scours the hills until he finds what is lost, for the sheep is of great value to him.

Surrounded by the wandering and lost sheep of society, Jesus makes clear that God pursues these very ones. Persistently, doggedly, God will remain on the trail in pursuit of the helpless, hopeless, and missing, no matter how expendable these seem to others.

To believe in God is to believe in the redemption of people. It is to believe that heaven's grace will not quit. Just because the pews of our churches are filled on Sunday morning with respectable neighbors does not mean God is happy with the number of those in his fold. He goes out into the wastelands—the highways and the byways—to pick up his children in his arms and carry them home. This is not a parable about a wayward sheep. This is a parable about an unrelenting God who will not rest until he finds those who are lost.

The second parable, about a woman's lost coin, is like the first and reinforces the same message. And as in the first parable, Jesus uses something familiar to his listeners but adds the now-expected twist. The Jewish rabbis had a saying about coins. They said a man must seek after God and his law with the intensity of searching for a lost coin. Jesus hijacks this proverb and makes clear that God chases after the law breakers, not necessarily the other way around.[3]

The woman's lost coin could be a denomination of money, representing a substantial sum in the economy of the day. The coin could be part of a larger collection of coins that made up a necklace or piece of jewelry with sentimental value.[4] Or maybe this lost coin was the woman's only savings. The exact nature of the lost item is unimportant. The point is that the woman lost something of consequence, and she turns her house upside down until she finds it.

While few of us are shepherds and we know little about chasing down a lost sheep, we can readily understand and identify with this woman's urgency. Anyone who has lost a diamond from its setting, a wedding band, or even a contact lens knows the frenzied rush of this kind of search. But as we know the panic of those moments, we also know the joy when we find what was lost, whether it be a sheep, a coin, or a set of keys.

Joy over finding what was lost is the punch line to these holy jokes Jesus tells.[5] The joke is on the Pharisees and teachers of the religious law once again. While they seethe with righteous indignation over Jesus' welcome of sinners, God could not be happier. "There is joy in the presence of God's angels when even one sinner repents," Jesus says (v. 10).

This is not the joy of singing, dancing angels, as some have misapplied the text. This is, rather, the joy of the One who shares company with the angels, God himself. He is celebrating in *their* presence, not they in his. While the religious folks wag their heads and mumble to one another about the inappropriateness of it all, God is the happiest reveler at the party of redemption.

After a heavy spring rain, my son Braden and I rescued a frog out of our garage. I easily caught him in my hands and then gently passed the little guy to Braden. We talked about the frog's warts, strong legs, and bulging eyes. After the brief science lesson, we set him free in the front yard. Braden followed his new friend around for a half hour. He tried to catch him, pet him, and steer him. He wanted the frog back in the garage—back in his hands—to do with him as he pleased. But this little frog would not oblige. In frustration, Braden finally lurched forward and crushed the little fellow beneath his foot.

I was horrified. I figured my wife and I were raising a sociopath at best or a serial killer at worst. Those are the guys who in their youth light fires and torture animals, right? When I could finally reel in my slack jaw, I asked him, "Why did you do that?"

His answer was as terrible as it was simple: "Because he wouldn't come to me."

Our five-year-old is now in therapy.

Some of us think that God has control issues similar to Braden's. If you don't stay one step ahead of him, leaping quickly from his crushing blow, God will maliciously scrub you into the dust. God will be patient for a while as he follows you about, but eventually he will catch up to you and squash you for every evil act you ever committed, every wrong thought that has crossed your mind, every stray look, and every missed Sunday service.

Maybe it stems from an anxious childhood, but we all too often see God for less than he is. Even more sinister than a misunderstanding of God, however, are those of us in the religious community who *want* God to be this way. Too often, we are not even subtle about it. We want God to crush the homosexual and the pro-choicer under his foot. We pray that he will wipe away with his righteous hand those of a theological or political bent different from our own. We wait in glee for the next natural disaster to strike so we can explain what group God is judging. We interpret the tragedy that befalls those with whom we disagree as some kind of personal vindication. We want sinners to quake in fear of the consuming God, so long, of course, as we get to define who the sinners are.

These conclusions say far less about what we think is right or wrong and more about who we wish God to be. Frighteningly, it reveals how hard of heart and how fallen we who preach God's forgiveness actually are. With one breath we say, "God loves you and has a wonderful plan for your life." With the next we point out, "You must come to God on our terms or he will smash the hell out of you."

In our rush to judgment, we fail to recognize that the ones we condemn are actually hungry for spirituality. They are wasting away with no real connection to God, maybe not even to other human beings. They need faith. They need hope. They need good news. But they cannot get to it. There are too many barriers, too many fences, too many dead ends—most of which are human-made. Too often the church itself is its own worst enemy and the biggest roadblock of all.

We have degraded Christianity into strong-armed morality or a list of dos and don'ts. We have lost the Christly ambition of tearing down the barriers that keep people from God. We have abandoned the invitation to people to come into the life-changing, life-forming journey of following Christ. Meanwhile, the God we use to threaten people isn't sitting in heaven with a menacing smile, delighting as people slide into the perdition of our imagination. He is among the desert hills, stretching out to put a hand around the scraggly leg of a lost sheep and pulling him to safety. He is dusting the floors of dark and filthy places, looking for the shine of someone more valuable to him than all the angels in heaven.

While the church offers conditional, bait-and-switch salvation, God untiringly presses on. He will not quit until he finds who he is looking for, even if that search takes him to places that bewilder the religious establishment.

The sheep-seeking shepherd, the broom-sweeping woman, and the sinner-saving God: all chased after something of great value. The sinners we so easily dismiss as hopeless subjects of divine wrath, God sees as invaluable children; children that his church may have given up on but children he cannot abandon. Thus, he will travel any distance, pay the highest price, bear all hardship, apply excruciating patience, and suffer the worst indignities to redeem one of his lost children.

How do I know he will go to such extremes? Because he has already done so.

These stories of lost things being recovered are more than the descriptions of a compassionate but faraway God. Jesus was describing his own work and ministry as God's Anointed One. Jesus had traveled the length of God's infinite universe, emptying himself of all prestige and reputation to sit at the supper table with scoundrels, sinners, and losers; to take into his body the worst the world could throw at him; and through a cross to seek and save what was lost. Remember, Jesus is not necessarily the pal of the church-going and respectable type. He is the friend of those who have fouled up their lives beyond human repair. He is the seeker who considers what is lost worthy of the price of rescue.

"This is Basher-52. I'm alive. Help."

Those were the most important words Captain Scott O'Grady ever spoke.

In summer 1995, O'Grady was a twenty-nine-year-old Air Force pilot enforcing the NATO no-fly zone over western Bosnia when his F-16 was cut in half by a surface-to-air missile. He safely ejected, parachuting nearly thirty thousand feet down into one of the more mountainous and heavily wooded regions of the country. Those hills and forests concealed him for the next six days as he survived on a diet of bugs and grass and drank rainwater squeezed out of his socks. Sleeping by day and traveling by night, he repeatedly attempted to contact NATO's air command with his emergency radio. When he finally made contact, American forces sprang immediately into action to rescue their downed pilot.

At 2:00 in the Bosnian morning, the American military began planning the hazardous mission. It took only minutes. While they could not invest much time, their resources more than made up for it. The rescue attempt spared nothing. Four dozen Marines, multiple CIA spy satellites, two CH-53 Sea Stallion helicopters, Cobra attack helicopters, Harrier jump jets, surveillance planes: in total, more than forty aircraft were deployed over the Adriatic and Bosnian airspace to ensure the safe rescue of a single lost pilot. The result was a textbook operation. Marines were on the ground no longer than two minutes, and the door to the rescue helicopter was open for only three seconds before Captain Scott O'Grady was yanked inside. The entire armada then covered the ninety-mile extraction back to home base at dragster speed, with O'Grady setting foot on the *U.S.S. Kearsarge* only five hours after his rescuers first heard his call for help.

Millions of dollars worth of aircraft was put at risk, not to mention the priceless value of dozens of soldiers and pilots. The operation jeopardized the strategies and policies of the United States government, if not all of NATO.

Was it worth it?

Ask the men who participated in the mission, who pulled their brother-in-arms to safety as he wept for joy in their embrace.

Ask the national security advisers who, on the other side of the world in Washington D.C., raised a toast and lit stogies in celebration of a life saved and a job well done.

Ask this pilot's wing mates who first recognized his voice as he called for help, who could barely fly their aircraft for the lumps in their throats and the tears filling their eyes.

Ask the O'Grady family, who days earlier had been visited by an Air Force chaplain with the news that their son and brother was missing, likely dead, but who now received word in the middle of the night that he was safe and sound.

Ask Captain Scott O'Grady himself. You will find him out there today, now a graduate of Dallas Theological Seminary, telling his story of loss and rescue.

He will tell you it was all worth the price.

Notes

1. Accessed July 16, 2008; to see where your favorite Bible verse ranks, go to www.top-verses.com.

2. Gerhard E. Lenski, *Power and Privilege: A Theory of Social Stratification* (New York: McGraw Hill, 1966), 215–81.

3. Leon Morris, *Luke,* rev. ed., Tyndale New Testament Commentaries (Grand Rapids: Eerdmans, 1995), 262.

4. William Barclay, *The Parables of Jesus* (Louisville: Westminster John Knox, 1999), 180.

5. The phrase "holy joke" is a favorite of Frederick Buechner. See his *Telling the Truth: The Gospel as Tragedy, Comedy, and Fairy Tale* (New York: Harper Collins, 1977), 68.

Reflection Questions

1. "Friend of sinners." That is the accusation regularly made against Jesus by his opponents. Would such an accusation stick against the church today? Why or why not?

2. How far should Christians go to tear down the walls between the church and outsiders? Who should move first or farthest: those inside the Christian community or those outside?

3. It is God, not necessarily his angels, who rejoices over the redemption of one lost soul. Why would God consider one person so worthy?

4. Which image is more familiar to you and why: the God who is aloof and angry or the God who chases after the lost?

5. What did it cost Jesus to redeem the lost? What will it cost the church to be Christ's partner in redemption? What are we willing to put at risk?

____

____

____

____

____

Chapter 11

Take Off Your Feet

> Wherever the Master traveled and ministered, two things inevitably happened: People's lives were changed, and the established religious order was upset.
>
> —Stephen Arterburn

Jesus told his listeners this story:

> A man had two sons. The younger son told his father, "I want my share of your estate now before you die." So his father agreed to divide his wealth between his sons.
>
> A few days later this younger son packed all his belongings and moved to a distant land, and there he wasted all his money in wild living. About the time his money ran out, a great famine swept over the land, and he began to starve. He persuaded a local farmer to hire him, and the man sent him into his fields to feed the pigs. The young man became so hungry that even the pods he was feeding the pigs looked good to him. But no one gave him anything.
>
> When he finally came to his senses, he said to himself, "At home even the hired servants have food enough to spare, and here I am dying of hunger! I will go home to my father and say, 'Father, I have sinned against both heaven and you, and I am no longer worthy of being called your son. Please take me on as a hired servant.'"
>
> So he returned home to his father. And while he was still a long way off, his father saw him coming. Filled with love and compassion, he ran to his son, embraced him, and kissed him. His son said to him, "Father, I have sinned against both heaven and you, and I am no longer worthy of being called your son."
>
> But his father said to the servants, "Quick! Bring the finest robe in the house and put it on him. Get a ring for his finger and sandals for his feet. And kill the calf we have been fattening. We must celebrate with a feast, for this son of mine was dead and has now returned to life. He was lost, but now he is found." So the party began.

> Meanwhile, the older son was in the fields working. When he returned home, he heard music and dancing in the house, and he asked one of the servants what was going on. "Your brother is back," he was told, "and your father has killed the fattened calf. We are celebrating because of his safe return."
>
> The older brother was angry and wouldn't go in. His father came out and begged him, but he replied, "All these years I've slaved for you and never once refused to do a single thing you told me to. And in all that time you never gave me even one young goat for a feast with my friends. Yet when this son of yours comes back after squandering your money on prostitutes, you celebrate by killing the fattened calf!"
>
> His father said to him, "Look, dear son, you have always stayed by me, and everything I have is yours. We had to celebrate this happy day. For your brother was dead and has come back to life! He was lost, but now he is found!" (Luke 15:11-32)

Bartolomé Estaban Murillo was a Baroque-era painter who lived in Seville in the 1600s, the golden age of Spanish painting. You may not recognize his name unless you are an artist or a collector, but you would certainly recognize much of his work. Most of his works are religious in nature: the *Immaculate Conception*, the *Vision of St. Anthony*, the *Adoration of the Magi*, *Baby Jesus giving Bread to the Pilgrims.* His works have been celebrated in the Louvre, scattered to museums around the world, and displayed in many European cathedrals among other places. His artistic career, however, began in a less than remarkable way.

In those days a young artist needed a patron, sponsor, or investor who believed in his talents and who would financially support his work. Murillo had no such patron. He was talented but unproven.

In his childhood home hung a picture of Jesus as a hardened, deadly serious shepherd boy. Jesus stood there in the frame with stiff, square shoulders, his shepherd's staff held tightly in his hand like a weapon. Behind his head was that tacky halo you found in all paintings of the period. Murillo detested the picture, which, ironically, would become his ticket to greatness.

One day, the young artist found himself at home alone. He removed the Jesus painting from its revered place on the wall, took out his paints and brushes, and went to work recasting the shepherd boy. When his parents returned, they were outraged, for Jesus was vandalized. The cynical face had been painted over with a goofy, amusing grin. Jesus' dark eyes were given the light of mischief. Murillo converted the horrible halo into an old, battered straw hat with wild, unruly hair sticking out all around. Jesus' shepherd's staff was turned into a crooked walking stick, and at his feet was not a pathetic, helpless lamb, but a wiggling puppy dog. Though a couple hundred years ahead of Mark Twain's time, the shepherd boy Jesus was transformed into Huckleberry Finn.

Murillo's father beat the boy nearly to death. Then the young artist was forced to carry the sacrilegious picture throughout the town as penance for his sin. A local artist saw the offending work, recognized Murillo's obvious talent, and became the boy's patron.[1]

Murillo's image of Jesus is one many of us love: the smiling, playful Jesus mingling among the sinners and the outcasts, the children and the marginalized, the sick and the poor. We have had enough of the incorrigible Jesus who is afraid to laugh, afraid to have a good time, who is somber, serious, and unapproachable. So we turn to the accepting, gracious Jesus. Thankfully this lively, alternative Jesus is not the invention of our imagination or the projection of our unfulfilled hopes. This Jesus is found in the Gospels, and he is certainly the Jesus who takes the Great Journey to Jerusalem in the book of Luke.

When we examine the canvas of a welcoming, compassionate Jesus, we find that Jesus is also painting a picture. With his words, actions, stories, and compassionate action, he paints a picture of who God really *is.* He is inviting us to know a smiling, welcoming, gracious God—a God who does not match many of the religious images we have been sold.

I am reminded of the small child who told his mother he was drawing a picture of God. She responded by saying, "But no one knows what God looks like."

The boy answered, "They will when I get finished."

The welcoming God is the main star of the Parable of the Prodigal Son. He is a Father who jumps from the front porch, forsaking his dignity to run and embrace a wayward child who has finally come home.

When I was a child, my church had an annual Bible trivia contest. It took place on a Sunday night and was a big deal. All the children from the "Primary" Sunday school class were lined up across the front of the church and given questions in game show style until only one child was left standing. That one was declared the winner. It was a fundamentalist's version of Confirmation, I suppose.

The first year I participated, I did well and was a finalist. But I lost the whole thing when I was asked an easy question: "What did God say when Moses discovered the burning bush?"

Talk about a give-me! I knew the answer and quoted it loudly: "Take off your *feet*; the place you are standing is holy ground." I was nervous, standing in front of the whole church and all. And knowing I was about to win must have severed the connection between my brain and my mouth. Something about "pride goeth before a fall" comes to mind.

"Are you sure?" the moderator asked me.

So I repeated it: "Take off your feet . . ."

I was gonged off the show in complete confusion. My mother explained to me afterward what I had said, and I was mortified.

My answer given that night some thirty years ago is more than accurate when related to the story of the prodigal son. This is sacred ground—some of the more sacred you will find—but its drastic message about the love and nature of God cuts our legs out from beneath us, challenging us to believe something invigoratingly different about who God is. It is holy ground, so take off your feet.

The story begins in a way that we sometimes ignore. While the younger prodigal son gets most of the attention, this is a story about two sons, not one.

But first things first: The younger comes to his father and demands his inheritance. By Jewish custom, this would have been a third of the father's estate and holdings, with the older brother getting two-thirds. While it was not completely unheard of to ask for the inheritance before a parent's death, it was calloused and disrespectful. For the younger son to make such a request, he was saying to his father, "I wish you were dead." This is a calculated act of abandonment. The younger son is taking what he believes to be his and turning his back on his father and family. The father, either graciously or foolishly, complies. He knows he cannot hold his son at home.

What happens next is well known. The now wealthy son moves away. He attracts fair-weather friends. He spends all his money. After he sells his remaining stock and pawns his Rolex, a famine strikes. Just when things could not get any worse, the stock market collapses, an economic recession sweeps the land, and the younger son is left with nothing. His end is the pigpen. He becomes a slave, raising swine and starving to death.

Jesus once again shows his ability as a skilled storyteller. For a Jew, nothing was worse than being a pig farmer. To this day, Jews still will not eat pork. It is against their religion. The prodigal represents a man who has slipped off the last rung of respectability, particularly for the son of a landowner. A like comparison, in our culture, would be for a Harvard-educated kid from the Hamptons to make a whirlwind tour of New York, Hollywood, and Los Angeles, but to end up on the south side of Chicago, strung out on heroine and meth, and selling sexual favors to pay the rent. This is the worst possible outcome for this young man.

Yet, he comes to his senses. Sitting in the pig slop one day, he has this epiphany: "I can starve to death back at home as easily as I can here. No, I wouldn't starve. My father's butler and maid have it better than me. I will go home and admit that I was wrong and ask dad if he will let me be the yard man."

Desperation drives him back home, and it is here that we can raise a protest: "The only reason he went home is because he had no place left to go. Had he been successful, he would have never thought about his father again. He did this only because he had to."

Well, yeah. That is the nature of being human, a nature we all share. We never repent—we never do anything of life-changing significance—until we have to. Now, this young man had to. There was no other choice. It was change or die. There was no shame in going home, but it would have been shameful and stubborn to remain where he was. His coming home, while a beautiful picture of the gospel, raises a further conflict within the story. How will his family receive him?

Do not let your familiarity with the biblical account defuse it of tension. This boy treated his father as if he was dead, and he wasted a third of the father's former estate. He was no less volatile or unpredictable than a contemporary rebellious teenager, and no more irresponsible than one of today's paparazzi-addicted Hollywood divas. This is no minor, let-bygones-be-bygones, inconsequential indiscretion of youth. This has been a calculated exercise in stupidity. But you would not know it by reading the rest of the story.

One afternoon the father sees a familiar gait in the stranger coming up the driveway, a driveway he has stared down for years. Even with the stooped shoulders and the head, hanging down as if glued to his chest, and the rags dangling from his body, the father recognizes his son. He leaps from the front porch swing, over the railing, and begins running to his long-lost boy. Before this kid can get out of his mouth his well-rehearsed confession of guilt, he has cast upon him a robe of honor covering his rags, a signet ring of authority placed on his filthy hand, the sandals of a wealthy land-owning son put on his slave's feet, and the fatted calf—a meal fit for a king, a meal large enough to feed the surrounding village—placed on the fire to cook.

With hardly a spoken word, just a humble walk and a broken heart, this wasteful, sinful child is restored to his place of sonship before he barely gets past the mailbox. He would say "I'm sorry," but he cannot get the words out of his mouth due to his father's kisses.

Jesus shows us a father—God in our story, who is gracious and forgiving. Who can be treated like he does not exist. Who can be written off as if he were dead. Who can have his resources wasted and entrusted talents squandered. Who can watch us gamble away our youth and destroy our bodies. Who can wait in the background while we sell our souls to the devil. And still—*still*—this God will meet you in the driveway with open arms before you even get inside the gate.

There are no sermons, no bitter "I-told-you-so," no lectures demanding that you'd better never let this happen again—only a merry "Welcome home!" and the mother of all parties to prove it.

In case you have not noticed, the party theme runs strong in Luke's Gospel. This is not a God who keeps his elevated seat in heaven. This is a Father who leaps at the chance to run to his sinful and errant children and say, "I'm so glad you're home!"

The 1992 Summer Olympics were held in Barcelona, Spain. Derek Redmon was a member of the British Olympic team and participated in the 400-meter race. Halfway through his race he tore his hamstring. He collapsed on the track as the other runners ran past. All his hopes of winning an Olympic medal vanished. Amazingly, Redmon got up and continued toward the finish line, dragging himself down the track. He was crying, the pain and disappointment evident on his face. The other runners were forgotten as the entire stadium erupted in support of a struggling Derek Redmon.

Then a second man appeared on the track. This man was no athlete. He was a graying, middle-aged man wearing a garish t-shirt and a "Just Do It" ball cap. He joined Redmon, put his arms around him, and walked with him down the track. The two pushed the medical and support personnel away until, together, they crossed the finish line. After the race, the identity of the man who came to Redmon's aid was discovered. It was Derek Redmon's father.

From eighteen rows up in the Barcelona stands, he had left his seat, weaved through the spectators and security guards, and negotiated a concrete barrier to make it to where his son had fallen on the track. When asked why he would take such a risk, he said, "When your son needs you, you don't need a security pass. He and I started this thing together and we finished it together."

Who won the 400 meters at the Barcelona Olympics? Nobody remembers. Honestly, outside a half dozen people in the world, nobody likely cares. But the world will remember Derek and Edward Redmon. Together, they won the hearts of all who watched that day, even though a piece of gold will never hang around either of their necks.

This is what God is like. He leaves his seat and runs to his children when they do not even have the strength to get up off the ground. We know God is like this because Jesus was like this, and this is the God he told us about.

How I wish the story ended right here. In fact, some commentators have opted for exactly that. They say the last half of this parable was inserted after the fact. That would be terribly convenient. We could then sing "Kum Bah Ya," stuff another slice of roasted veal into our mouths, and lift a toast to all is well that ends well. But remember how this story begins: "A man had two sons." The younger one is back home, under the father's roof. Where is the second son, or I should say the first son? The missing character is the older brother.

The elder son is where good sons are always found: he is coming in from the fields where he has worked hard on his father's farm all day. What does he find? A party! He parks the John Deere tractor in the barn and uncouples the hay baler. He walks over to the mudroom to wash his sweaty, sunburned face and remove his boots from his sore feet. He drains the cooler of a long drink of cold water, turns to one of the farm hands, and asks, "What's going on at the house?"

Then he gets the happy retort: "Your little brother, filthy and broken but alive, has returned home safe and sound." Big brother does not receive this report as good news, not remotely. He is mad as hell and refuses to come into the house. Again we are forced into conflict: how will the father in our story react? Graciously, the father goes out to meet his firstborn son.

Earlier, the father jumped from the front porch and ran to his prodigal and carried him joyously home. Now he slips out the back door to attempt to do the same for his oldest. We know who the father is in this story. He is God. We know who the prodigal is. He is the sinner, the tax collector, the undesirable that Jesus always seemed to champion. This much is clear. Who then is the older brother?

He is the Pharisee and the expert in the religious law. Again Jesus puts his antagonists in the story. The religious leaders are the muttering, complaining older brothers who stand outside the house of God and refuse to share space with the sinners and outlaws who are actually their brothers and sisters.

Jesus, while being consummately hard on the religious crowd, here strikes a change of tone. Jesus gives us a God who is as tender and gracious with the religious as he is with the prodigal. The father goes out and pleads with his son to come in. This God, this kingdom, is about bringing the *entire* family together under heaven's roof, for there is room for all.

Yes, the prodigals must repent of their wayward ways and come home, but the older brothers—the religious—must repent as well: of pride, arrogance, and a sense of superiority. Only then can we be the family of God, where brothers and sisters of all extremes realize that we must walk through the same door to join the party, and that door is the grace of the Father.

The older brother finds this solidarity nearly impossible. He protests loudly, furiously, and accurately: "He has embarrassed the family. He embarrasses me. He has squandered your wealth on prostitutes, drugs, and God knows what else. He has ruined your portfolio, the family's finances, and your good name. He is irresponsible and self-centered, nothing but a damn fool. And you, you let him off the hook by throwing a party just because he comes crawling home when he's got nothing left to waste and nowhere else to go."

I sympathize with the older brother because he tells the truth. His accusations are absolutely correct. Then, in verse 29, he says something else absolutely true: "All these years I've been slaving for you."

Here we arrive at the real source of the older brother's and, thus, religion's anger. Do not miss this. The good son, the older brother, hard-working religionist that he is, has been faithful, meticulous, dedicated, and committed to the work of the father. Yet the elder defines his relationship with his father as *slavery*. He has done his duty even when others would not. He has soldiered on while some in the family did nothing but have a good time. He has pushed his rock up the hill with no one to lift even a finger of assistance. And he has done all of this not as a son, but as a slave. He has labored as a minimum-wage employee, punching the clock, completing his "to-do" list, and fulfilling his obligations. Yet, he has not accepted his role in the family. He does not see himself as his father's child.

The reason the older brother was so scandalized by his father's actions, the reason he could not understand or accept what his father was doing, was that he did not know who his father really was. He stood at a distance, working the fields, but never accepted his father's embrace.

Are we any different? We cry out in protest when some tarnished sinner has a conversion experience, and our protest is the same as the older brother's. It is not so much a protest against the prodigal as it is a protest against God. God is not being fair when he lets sinners off the hook, while we are the ones who have never stopped slaving for him. It is not fair. Our Father's reaction is, of course, "This is who I am! I forgive and embrace my children when they come home. This is what I do, and so should you! This is not 'my son.' This is 'your brother.'"

John Steele was my first principal. Broad-shouldered and tall, he was the kind of man you might see wearing football pads on Sunday afternoon, not one walking the hallways of an elementary school. To go with his massive frame, he had a thunderous voice and a tight Zorro-style moustache. Long, curly black locks flowing down his back completed the intimidating package. Every day on bus duty, standing there on the sidewalk, he looked out across his world like some kind of god straddling Mount Olympus, ready to call down fire from heaven. To a tiny first grader, he might as well have been a god, because holy smokes could he bring the fire.

See, it was rumored, though never truly confirmed nor contradicted, that John Steele possessed in his office an electric paddle. The story goes that he plugged it into the wall, let it warm up, and then summarily attached it to the seat of your britches. We all knew there was some kind of hellacious torture device behind his office door. What else could squeeze tears and wails from the eyes and mouths of the school's most wayward little boys? No one spoke openly about the matter. Like Harry Potter's Lord Voldemort, John Steele's paddle was the instrument of punishment too terrifying to be named.

John Steele fit my elementary image and idea of God. In my imagination, God was a tall, dark, brooding figure with a deep baritone voice. Twisting the end of his moustache with one hand and twirling his paddle with the other, he watched over his world like an aloof schoolmaster on playground duty.

Don't play too long or too rough. It is sure to draw his irritated attention.

Don't break the rules. He is liable to break his paddle over your backside.

And certainly don't enjoy yourself or appear too happy. A smile on your face will be grounds enough for being dragged away for a beating.

My parents, my own fears, my pastor's sermons: I suppose all of these conspired together to give God this image. It has taken me most of my adult life to shake it off. But now, I no longer believe in this manufactured image of God—God as a terrorizing bully. I do not believe God is irrepressibly angry or that he peers out of heaven waiting to thump us on the head with a big stick. I used to think this way, and worse, but not anymore. The infuriated mad-as-hell and I'm-not-going-to-take-it-anymore God of my childhood does not match up with the God revealed to us in Jesus the Christ.

This God revealed to us in Jesus is a gracious, barrier-breaking, party-inviting, sin-forgiving lover of men and women. This God does not throw the unrighteous out on their ears. He invites them to the banquet table. This God does not lock the door on his broken prodigal or his arrogant religious children. He restores their place and dignity in the family. This is not a God clutching white-knuckled and angrily to a wooden paddle. This is a vulnerable God whose open hands were nailed to a wooden cross.

My image of John Steele was wrong. In adulthood I have found him to be wonderfully normal. He has hobbies, friends, a wife and family (I even baptized his nephew—weird, huh?). And I discovered that he does not eat kindergartners for breakfast, and his paddle was never electrified. Refreshingly, he is someone you would love to have over to watch the game and have a beer. To get to know my once intimidating principal, I only had to get past my fears and suspicions. All those times he watched over us in the hallways, and the cafeteria, and the playground, his intention was never to punish or harm us. Rather, he had our best interests at heart. He actually loved—and still loves—the children under his care. In the end, that's not so hard to believe about principals or about God.[2]

Jesus' invitation is for us to flush away these horrible misconceptions about who we think God is and to discover a God worth believing, worth worshiping, worth loving. Jesus' invitation is to find our Father, the Father of both older and younger, the religious and the prodigal. For in the end, the many differences between the older and younger brothers are merely cosmetic. Scratch the skin of these siblings and you find the same thing.

Both have avoided their father's rule, one through rebellion, the other through resentment.

Both have committed injustice against his love, one by running, the other by losing himself in self-created slavery.

Both have insulted their father's reputation, one by treating him as if he were dead, the other by never getting to know him.

Both have lived their lives far from home, one literally, the other figuratively.

There is only one real difference between the two: The prodigal, for all his faults, somewhere in that distant pigpen came to the realization that he was not a slave but the son of a loving father, and he said, "I will arise. I will go home. He will embrace me in his arms." Then the prodigal went home. The elder of the two had yet to come to this understanding, still seeing his father as a taskmaster, as hard and emotionless as a stone. So instead of running to his father's arms, he relied upon himself and his own status as the "good" son and stood outside the party.

As this masterful parable closes, the sun dips low to touch the horizon with scarlet light. The coolness of the coming night is already in the air. In the background we hear music playing, shouting and singing around the dance floor, champagne bottles opening, glasses, forks and spoons clanging. And in the backyard the older son stands, his hands trembling with rage and indecision, the crickets chirping in the freshly cut hay. The father, his cheeks wet with tears, begs the boy to come in and enjoy the party, to rejoin the family, because there is no other real choice.

Did the older brother come in? We are not told. Jesus leaves it for us to wonder, and he leaves it as an invitation for us all.

Come to the party.

Rejoin the family.

Walk boldly through the welcome door of grace.

From the muddy pigpens of sinful rebellion and the sweat-laden fields of religious obligation, the Father says, "Come home. Make room, children, for your brothers and your sisters, in the house I have made; a house called the kingdom of God."

Notes

1. Adapted from Michael Frost, *Jesus the Fool* (Sydney: Albatross, 1994), 19.

2. Ronnie McBrayer, *Keeping the Faith: Passages, Proverbs, Parables* (Freeport: Leaving Salem, 2008), 134–36.

Reflection Questions

1. The Prodigal Son story is actually about two sons. Why does the older of the two brothers in the story get little to no attention?

2. The only reason the prodigal went home to his father was desperation. Is this a credible motive? Why or why not?

3. Explain whether or not you think the older brother was right to feel angry when he realized his younger sibling had returned home.

4. Slavery to sin or slavery to religious obligation: is there any real difference between the two?

5. Are you afraid of God? Why or why not?

____

____

____

____

____

Chapter 12

Imagine

You must wager. It is not optional. You are embarked.
—Blaise Pascal

Jerome Kerviel is a name you may not recognize. Had he not made the largest individual financial blunder in the history of world banking, he would still be sitting in front of his computer monitor at Paris's Société Générale Bank today, trading stocks. But that is no longer the case.

This young computer genius committed a series of terribly complex, high stakes futures trades. Things started small—a few million here, a few million there, and with substantial success. He made his employer millions of dollars as 2007 ended and 2008 began. But in January 2008, while U.S. markets enjoyed the extended Martin Luther King Jr. holiday weekend, the European financial markets shook and shuttered, losing five billion Euros in value. Much of the responsibility for this loss has been laid at Kerviel's feet.

Société Générale called Kerviel a "rogue trader" without authorization for his actions and with an agenda of his own. Of course Kerviel claimed that he did what he did with the full knowledge and endorsement of his immediate supervisors. Regardless, Kerviel's bets came crashing down as he could no longer hedge his losses. Those losses were astronomical: at one point Kerviel had almost $78 billion at play in the world markets, and in the end his speculation cost one of France's most prestigious blue-chip banks more than $7.9 billion. Yes, that is billion with a "b"—just gone. Think about that next time you have a bad quarter with your 401K.

The investigation into the entire incident will continue for years. The financial recovery will be lengthy, more heads will roll, and the embarrassment for many will be unbearable. But Mr. Kerviel has already moved on to better things. He has secured new employment with a company that specializes in computer and financial security measures. It sounds like a good match.

Jesus' stories are always relevant. Were his tales spoken centuries ago or written in yesterday's newspaper copy? Compare the above story about Kerviel with the Parable of the Dishonest Manager in Luke 16:

> Jesus told this story to his disciples: "There was a certain rich man who had a manager handling his affairs. One day a report came that the manager was wasting his employer's money. So the employer called him in and said, 'What's this I hear about you? Get your report in order, because you are going to be fired.'
>
> "The manager thought to himself, 'Now what? My boss has fired me. I don't have the strength to dig ditches, and I'm too proud to beg. Ah, I know how to ensure that I'll have plenty of friends who will give me a home when I am fired.'
>
> "So he invited each person who owed money to his employer to come and discuss the situation. He asked the first one, 'How much do you owe him?' The man replied, 'I owe him 800 gallons of olive oil.' So the manager told him, 'Take the bill and quickly change it to 400 gallons.'
>
> "'And how much do you owe my employer?' he asked the next man. 'I owe him 1,000 bushels of wheat,' was the reply. 'Here,' the manager said, 'take the bill and change it to 800 bushels.'
>
> "The rich man had to admire the dishonest rascal for being so shrewd. And it is true that the children of this world are more shrewd in dealing with the world around them than are the children of the light. Here's the lesson: Use your worldly resources to benefit others and make friends. Then, when your earthly possessions are gone, they will welcome you to an eternal home." (Luke 16:1-9)

This is one of Jesus' more perplexing stories. It is about as easy to unravel as following the electronic trail of a renegade stock trader. Its complexity is found in its vagueness. It is not abundantly clear what point Jesus is making with this story. Good Samaritans, prodigal sons, great banquets: we follow those easy enough. But here Jesus makes a seedy, irresponsible, if not embezzling, day trader an example for his disciples to follow. This tale is a tough nut to crack.

We are awfully deep in this book to address the best approach for interpreting Jesus' parables, but a brief look at method will help us here. Michael Ball, in his book *The Radical Stories of Jesus,* provides a useful guide for studying Jesus' parables. Among other things, he suggests that the reader attempt to remove all presuppositions when coming to the text (though he admits this is impossible), and that he or she read the parable carefully, watching out for cultural peculiarities and the unexpected.[1]

Even then, when we take great interpretive care, Ball is right to point out that the reader will not always arrive at a definite conclusion about the parable's meaning. That there is just "one original meaning which we can recover, and that this is also Jesus' intended meaning is very questionable," says Ball.[2] See, the Hebrew word for "parable" can also be translated "riddle." Sometimes the stories of Jesus are exactly that: riddles. The closest a reader can come to a definitive conclusion is the complex conversation that takes place between Jesus, the Gospel writer, the original audience, hundreds of years of interpretive history, and the reader all sitting at the same table in noisy dialogue. Listening for a clear voice is sometimes harder than we wish to imagine.

Still, the parables speak. With every new reader, these stories of Jesus echo new sounds, and each generation must listen again for the voice of Christ in their own particular context. Ball writes, "There seems to be no reason why the Spirit should not continue to use these same parables in new ways. The Spirit speaks afresh to those who have ears to hear."[3]

With all this said, we can approach this Parable of the Dishonest Manager, maybe not with confidence, but at least a bit more prepared. We can set aside any idea of deducing from Jesus' words here a single meaning, because for most of Christian history, this parable, as much as any Jesus told, is without consensus. It is, to use Ball's phrase, "an open-ended medium" in which the listener's response is of the essence.[4] The "correct" interpretation, then, depends largely on where this story finds the reader.

So, while it is uncertain where this story finds you, it is easy to see where the story finds the main character: in big trouble. The manager of the rich man's affairs has been wasteful in his administration. The word used by Jesus in this story is the same one used to describe the "prodigal" son. The manager has been careless and irresponsible. His paperwork has been sloppy. He has kept inconsistent hours and padded his expense report. Maybe he was not above taking a bribe under the table. No longer able to hedge his bets, the manager's head rolls. He is fired. But before he cleans out his desk, he scrambles for a solution. The manager invites all of the rich man's debtors to a meeting. Individually he goes over their accounts and begins drastically discounting their debts, up to fifty percent in some cases.

What if the loan officer at your bank summoned you to her office for a meeting about your mortgage and car loans?

"What is the balance on your mortgage?" she asks you.

"About $180,000," you say.

"Let's make that $90,000. Just sign right here. And what about your automobile? I see you still owe $14,000 on it. We're going to rewrite the loan for $7,000. Is that satisfactory?"

Most of us would ask questions, but probably not for long. We would sign our names on the dotted line and bolt out the door before she changed her mind about this personalized bailout plan.

This is exactly what the manager in Jesus' parable does. He does not doctor the books before he leaves. No, far more drastic than that, he replaces all the original contracts. The rich man, his boss, will now have no recourse to collect the original amounts owed to him, for those amounts and the contracts binding his debtors to them have found their way to the office shredder. Even if the rich man presses his debtors into court, they will simply produce the signed, sealed, and airtight documents now in their possession. If only Jerome Kerviel had been so clever.

Jesus commends this audacious cleverness as worthy of replication, and his commendation has wadded the shorts of more than one biblical interpreter trying to make sense of this parable. "How can Jesus make a lawbreaker the hero of the story?" seems to be the quarrel. Well, why not? He does it all the time. Samaritans, tax collectors, prodigal sons, notorious sinners: Jesus is not afraid to put the sleaziest bunch in his stories, and not just include them as background characters, but as drum majors leading the parade into the kingdom of God.

But to get around the ethical difficulties of this parable, some commentators have suggested that the manager is not being dishonest with his discounts at all. They propose that he is cutting out his own commission, or that he is canceling the exorbitant interest rate on the loans made by the rich man.[5] It was a violation of Mosaic Law to charge credit-card-style interest rates, though plenty of possible bookkeeping gymnastics helped circumvent this little difficulty. These commentators want to see the manager in the story, as his back is now pressed against the wall, getting religion and doing what is right. They say he is bringing the books into compliance. I think this approach involves a bit of interpretive aerobics in an attempt to protect an overly sanctified image of Jesus.

It seems better, at least more honest, to see the manager for what he really is: a crook, a snake, one who will do whatever it takes to maintain the lifestyle his wasteful ways have made for him. Should we really think that one who has made his living breaking and bending the rules will now enforce them as he picks up his pink slip at the door? No. Even if he has seen the light, ethically he is still in the wrong for rewriting his boss's business contracts with debtors. He is still breaking and bending the rules. There is no way around it. Yet Jesus says, "The rich man had to admire the dishonest rascal for being so shrewd."

The rich man was outplayed, something the poor agricultural-based listeners of Jesus would have loved hearing. He attempted to achieve "justice" by firing this crook, but all the rich man did was make his former manager the most sought-after golf partner at the country club. "Touché," can be his only response.

Meanwhile, the dishonest manager accomplishes his goal. Living the high life makes for soft hands and love handles, so he cannot get out and dig ditches, and he will not lower himself to begging. But he will have to do neither. All the Wall Street buddies he helped with his shifty accounting will line up to give him a job. Remember: what would you do to help the banker who cut your mortgage in half? For this scoundrel, crime paid quite nicely.

Jesus, in the midst of the crooks and the confusion, thankfully helps us understand this parable. He says, "The children of this world are more shrewd in dealing with the world around them than are the children of the light. *Here's the lesson*: Use your worldly resources to benefit others and make friends. Then, when your earthly possessions are gone, they will welcome you to an eternal home" (vv. 8b-9; emphasis added).

We must remember Michael Ball's instruction to look for the unexpected in the parables of Jesus, because the honesty of the manager's actions is insignificant. This is not a parable intended as a lecture on business ethics or a sermon on morality. Rather, it is a rousing call to action: use the gifts, positions, influence, and resources you have been given to help others, to lighten your neighbor's load, to "make friends," and to ensure a warm welcome into the kingdom of God.

"If a crook can make such good connections that he is rescued from poverty," Jesus seems to ask, "can you not connect to others with the gospel?" Jesus does not imply that we can "buy our way" into the kingdom or that others should be bought, but he makes it crystal clear that what we do with our lives will determine how and who will receive us there.

My friend Michael Belk is the creative force behind *Journeys with the Messiah.* For thirty years Michael has worked as a photographer and producer in the fashion worlds of New York, Los Angeles, and beyond. Russell

Athletics, Ralph Lauren, Calvin Klein, Cutter Buck: he has worked with some big names. But Michael, upon coming to the end of himself and to Christ in mid-life, recently stepped away from his career to pursue *Journeys*, an exhibition of audacious fine art images intended to challenge the viewer with all kinds of creative twists and to invite others to pursue this Messiah.[6]

The questions that have stuck like splinters in Michael's brain, that have pushed him along on his journey, that precipitated this entire project, and that have dogged him in recent years are "What did you do with all that I gave you? The gifts? The time? The money? Did you use it all for yourself? Did you share it with others?"

We should all be dogged by these questions and respond with our own answers:

Those of us who write.

Who teach children.

Who take photographs.

Who paint or play music.

Who build homes or fix toilets.

Who trade stocks or make loans.

Who fix cars, serve coffee, care for the sick, or launder clothes.

What did you do with all that he gave you? The gifts? The time? The money? Did you use it all for yourself? Did you share it with others? It is right that these questions aren't just about wealth—not at all—but about *everything* you have been given: your talents, your job, your connections, your interactions with others, your website, your business, your conversations—everything! This does not mean you give all of these a "Christian" label, and we all put little fish symbols on our business cards or bumpers. Lord, please no. It means we live as servants of Christ in submission to the kingdom of God, even if we are never given the opportunity to name it "Christianity."

We could read this parable as a word picture for Jesus' words from the Sermon on the Mount. There he said, "Don't store up treasures here on earth, where moths eat them and rust destroys them, and where thieves break in and steal. Store your treasures in heaven, where moths and rust cannot destroy, and thieves do not break in and steal" (Matt 6:19-20).

These treasures, however, are not material, for such things have no value in God's kingdom. These treasures are people. The "friends" who wait for us with open arms in the presence of God are those who arrived there because of our efforts. Efforts alive with creativity, imagination, and, yes, even a bending of the establishment's rules and expectations. We are called to live with a reckless ingenuity that will convert the physical and material resources in our hands into eternal friendships in the kingdom of God.

This "storing up in heaven," or "making of spiritual friends," is not primarily a ministerial function. Too much of the church operates with a false dichotomy that puts the ordained clergy in the major league of ministry while the "laity" plays in the minors, or more accurately, sits in the bleachers and watches. This ought not be.

A friend said to me recently that all pastors should wear a t-shirt that says, "Water Boy," for that is the pastoral function: to run out on the field where God's people sweat and struggle and give them the refreshment, equipment, and encouragement they need to stay in the game.

If there is a dichotomy at all in the New Testament, it is the inverse of how we have understood and practiced it. Big-league ministry is accomplished by those actually playing the game, not by we who spend the bulk of our time reading theology, preaching sermons, and leading prayer meetings. The creative opportunity to impact the lives of others is in your hands and in the hands and hearts of others just like you.

This is a parable supremely about creativity and imagination—your creativity and imagination. Jesus compares the dishonest manager to the "people of the light" and determines that Jerome Kerviel has more vision and resourcefulness than a Christian universe filled with Kenneth and Gloria Copelands. Again, this ought not be.

We have the most courageous and creative message the world has ever heard. Surely we have more imagination than it takes to produce schmaltzy coffee mugs, "Jesus" bumper stickers, Christian t-shirts, and the *Left Behind* series. Somewhere in our individual and collective hearts there must be an artistic imagination that will enable us to connect with and aid those in need of God's good news in Christ. If the world can invent a million new ways to steal, pilfer, or make money every day, then maybe we can flesh out and express with our lives, work, play, and worship fresh ways to bring the kingdom of God to bear in this world.

I pastor a small church in northwest Florida. Let me clarify two words in that previous sentence. First, "pastor" is my function, not necessarily my title. That suits me fine, and I try to be a good water boy to those laboring in the trenches. Second, there is the word "church." The word has been butchered, so we are not always comfortable using it when communicating with others. Yes, we are a church, but we are not very structured. Rather, our little congregation is a place where Baptists, Catholics, Lutherans, Anglicans, Nazarenes, Methodists, and those who don't know what to call themselves come together, not in some interdenominational goulash or in protest against institutionalism. We come together recognizing that there is no hope in organized religion; there is only hope in Christ.

It is an edgy place, a bit prickly and frustrating for some. Not because we do strange things in our worship service—we are a fairly mellow group—but because we do not possess many of the Christian comforts church shoppers look for: organization, membership, age-graded programs to meet the needs of everyone from the cradle to the nursing home, well-polished worship services, or capital campaigns to build the next big building. We don't have a marketing strategy, an information brochure, and, until recently, not even a website. All we have is word of mouth and our lives in the community. That is by intention. If we cannot say it with the lives we live, then we cannot say it.

But here is the bright side to such an approach: The people who have come together in community at this little church need a place to get well. They have histories of hurting and brokenness and need grace. They are seekers on a journey they do not have the questions for, much less the answers. They are weary of being castigated for their doubts and questions, weary of attempts to fix, trick, or manipulate them. In short, they have had it with religion—even Christianity as they have practiced it—but know that faith in Christ and the unique, matchless truth he provides is still worth holding on to. It is the most unique group I have ever been a part of, and I am grateful to tote their water.

A small group of these unique people sat together one night trying to figure out what to do with some money. There is nothing especially distinct about that. Every church has to figure it out. But what happened on this night was unusual. The group decided to break the bank—to give away every penny the church had. When the church began, we wanted to spend our resources along three lines: a third for our internal operations, paying the rent, and keeping the lights on; a third to support pastors and needed ministers; and a third on community outreach, assistance to the poor, and mission to the world. As of the night of this meeting, we were not there yet. We had not been able to give to mission and the community the way we would like.

Susan, the woman who kept the church's books, said emphatically, "We've got to give this money away."

I had never heard the designated money-changer in the church talk like that. It has been my experience that the church treasurer wants to horde all the church's money away somewhere, like she is saving it for her grandchildren's trust fund. I was proud to hear this, but not quite ready for the implications. After all, churches need a bit of cushion, don't they? A buffer between them and an emergency? Selfishly, I actually thought, "If you fools give away all our money, how will I get paid next month?" But creativity and risk prevailed over sensibility and caution.

A few weeks later I stood before the congregation with a stack of plain white envelopes. Each envelope had inside it a $100 bill. In total, it was every dollar we had. As worshipers came forward for Communion that Sunday, they were given an envelope: adults, children, first-time attendees, guests from out of town—everyone. When the last envelope was handed out, we were broke.

With the envelope came a charge: "This money is not yours. It belongs to you no more than it belongs to the church. It is God's money, so let it loose. Give it away in the name of Christ, no strings attached. Give it to a ministry that needs it. Donate it to build houses for those without shelter. Buy food for a family who is hungry. Leave it as a tip for the waitress whom you discover is a single mom working two jobs to support her kids. Give it to the family down the street whose kids need shoes. Mail it to that elderly woman you know who cannot afford her medications. Buy the gas for that single dad so he can get to work this week. Send it overseas. Help replenish our community food banks. Buy Bibles to give to those who need one. The possibilities are limited only by your imagination, but give it away."

Something incredible happened that day and in the weeks that followed. People began to think about others more than usual, and how they could creatively and joyfully give away a bit of the blessing they had received. But the overwhelming sentiment was this: "Do you really trust me to do this?"

I had to face, with more than a little embarrassment, what I already knew: the church and its leadership have done such a lousy job of fostering our people's imaginations, that when given an opportunity to express themselves in creative ministry, they cannot believe it. We are failing to plant in those who call themselves followers of Christ the response-*ability* to be the risk-taking people of God.

I will not make further suggestions for you here. You have to work that out on your own. But I will return to Michael Ball. Remember what he said about Jesus' parables? The stories of Jesus are "an open-ended medium" that require the listener to interact and respond. The "correct" interpretation of the parable depends largely on where the story finds you, the reader.

So imagine. Let your mind go. Chase down and explore those ideas too big, too bizarre, too risky and unconventional to be acceptable. And do them.

Religion has enough rationality, enough order, and enough predictability. But life is not lived that way, and our Lord certainly did not call us to live that way. Jesus did not say, "Follow me and I will make you feel good. Follow me and I will make you into a moral, upstanding citizen in the community. Follow me and I will make you a respectable church member. Follow me and I will make you an admired contributor of the community." He said, "Follow me, deny yourself, take up your cross, and seize the path that leads to resurrection."

We are not a people intended to play it safe. The church is dying for dangerous creativity, for death-defying purpose, and for foolish jeopardy. Let us not die for lack of these things. Let us go live them.

You have nothing to lose, and your neighbors may have eternity to gain.

Notes

1. Michael Ball, *The Radical Stories of Jesus; Interpreting the Parables Today* (Oxford: Regent's, 2000), 97–111.

2. Ibid., 92.

3. Ibid., 94.

4. Ibid., 82.

5. See chapter 4 above, "A Fool and His Money," where I discuss interest-charging practices of first-century Palestine.

6. Please take a look at Michael's imagination at www.journeyswiththemessiah.com.

Reflection Questions

1. Michael Ball suggests that parables are best interpreted after the reader removes all presuppositions. How, if at all, is this possible?

2. How do Jesus' parables defy easy or one-meaning explanations?

3. Does the description "water boy" ascribed to pastors and ministers strike you as accurate? How would you describe the pastoral function?

4. I describe our congregation giving away everything we had in the bank. Was this good stewardship? What would it take for your church to do something like this?

5. What is the difference between responsibility and response-ability?

____

____

____

____

____

Chapter 13

The Burning Hell

> I'm not a bad guy. I work hard. I love my kids. So why should I spend half my Sunday hearing about how I'm going to hell?
>
> —Homer Simpson

Years ago my sister sent me an e-mail that I have saved because it is so unbelievably coincidental that it has to be true.[1]

A business man from Wisconsin went on a business trip to Louisiana. When he arrived at his hotel he plugged in his laptop and sent a short message to his wife who was back at home. Her name was Jennifer Johnson, and her e-mail was JennJohn@world.net. In his haste to get an e-mail to his wife, he mistyped her address. His message went instead to JeanJohn@world.net, a Mrs. Jean Johnson.

Jean Johnson was the wife of a minister who had recently died, and who had just been buried on that same day. The minister's wife opened her e-mail, read the message, and promptly fainted.

It read, "Arrived safely; but it sure is hot down here."

A light-hearted beginning to this parable of Jesus may be the best approach. For it is a heavy subject: the condemnation of the afterlife, the suffering of the great beyond, the dark netherworld, what my children appropriately call "the H-word." Hell.

Hell is the big stick, the heavy ammunition pulled out by preachers, pundits, and parents when the going really gets tough. We threaten people with all manner of trouble and judgment to keep them on the straight and narrow. While we may begin with lesser efforts, when these fail, we unhinge the Damocles Sword of burning hellfire on wayward sinners. It is a favorite tool of religion, regardless of what religion we are talking about.

When I was a child of five or so, I saw a movie at church. This was unusual. Watching movies was right up there with card playing, dancing, and whiskey drinking on the taboo list. These were things in which a decent fundamentalist did not participate. We hated these things with about as much passion as we hated William T. Sherman, Yankees, and Catholics. Seeing how these were all tools of the devil (movies, card playing, dancing whiskey drinking, Sherman, Yankees, and Catholics, that is), a movie at church was unheard of. Even as a kindergartner I knew this.

So on a Sunday night in the summer of 1975, the Glade Baptist Church was filled to overflowing to watch a film written by, produced by, and even starring Mississippi evangelist Estus Pirkle. The name of the movie was *The Burning Hell.*[2] The acting was terrible and the special effects were third rate at best. But the film's effect on me has been lifelong. That one movie, more than any other single event, birthed in me a religious-driven fear: God was out to get me, and he was eager to burn my backside given the opportunity.

I can remember my father standing outside the church, the doors and windows kept open to let the summer breezes pass through. He had stepped out with me, as I was clinging to his neck with my face buried in his shoulder weeping and begging to go home. Inside the church, horrific scenes played of children and parents being torn from their families. Other worse sinners like hippies and bikers were handed over to the devil, and all the condemned languished about in the flames. At the end of the film, there was, of course, the proverbial invitation to give your heart to Jesus and avoid said destruction. This seemed to be the main point of showing the film: be afraid, be very afraid.

I don't know how many repented that night. By the time the invitation hymn was sung, I was exhausted with fear and my father had finally taken me to the car. Those of us forced to watch that film thirty years ago ought to get into heaven just for having endured it.

Many of the church's doctrinal conclusions about hell, and certainly Estus Pirkle's interpretation of the same, are based largely on a dozen or so verses from Luke 16 and the parable about Lazarus and the Rich Man. As in other places along this journey with Jesus, the Christian community has not been as responsible with this story as we could and should have been. It is a terrible parable about judgment, yes, but as we will see, it is not explicitly about heaven, hell, or how to get into one and avoid the other. It is more about entering and embracing the way of Christ and joining Jesus on that Way, living out his sweeping message of the kingdom of God.

> Jesus said, "There was a certain rich man who was splendidly clothed in purple and fine linen and who lived each day in luxury. At his gate lay a poor man named Lazarus who was covered with sores. As Lazarus lay there

> longing for scraps from the rich man's table, the dogs would come and lick his open sores.
>
> "Finally, the poor man died and was carried by the angels to be with Abraham. The rich man also died and was buried, and his soul went to the place of the dead. There, in torment, he saw Abraham in the far distance with Lazarus at his side.
>
> "The rich man shouted, 'Father Abraham, have some pity! Send Lazarus over here to dip the tip of his finger in water and cool my tongue. I am in anguish in these flames.'
>
> "But Abraham said to him, 'Son, remember that during your lifetime you had everything you wanted, and Lazarus had nothing. So now he is here being comforted, and you are in anguish. And besides, there is a great chasm separating us. No one can cross over to you from here, and no one can cross over to us from there.'
>
> "Then the rich man said, 'Please, Father Abraham, at least send him to my father's home. For I have five brothers, and I want him to warn them so they don't end up in this place of torment.'
>
> "But Abraham said, 'Moses and the prophets have warned them. Your brothers can read what they wrote.'
>
> "The rich man replied, 'No, Father Abraham! But if someone is sent to them from the dead, then they will repent of their sins and turn to God.'
>
> "But Abraham said, 'If they won't listen to Moses and the prophets, they won't listen even if someone rises from the dead.'" (Luke 16:19-31)

This uniquely Lucan story appears to be a popular Egyptian folktale of the period that Jesus adapted for his own use.[3] In Jesus' version we are first introduced to a man named Lazarus, the only character in any of Jesus' stories who is given an actual name. Here, we learn more than just his name. He is a crippled, starving beggar thrown out on the street every day to plead and beg for charity. It is likely that a neighbor or someone with a little pity drug him there each day or tumbled him off their donkey just to get rid of him. Who knows how he got home each evening, or if he even had a home to which to return? He is in a miserable, helpless condition.

To make matters worse, his body is covered with ulcerating, open sores. He is so vulnerable he cannot even keep the dogs off. They come and lick his wounds. These are not sweet little puppies you would see at the Westminster Kennel Show or posing in a Eukanuba advertisement. These are vicious, mangy street mutts as hungry for a meal as Lazarus. Reading the text, we are compelled to believe that these dogs might think of Lazarus as that next meal, with his open sores as appetizers before the main course. Lazarus suffers like this every day, just outside the gated home of a certain Rich Man.

This Rich Man, character number two, lives in a resort community outfitted with security guards, video surveillance, homeowner covenants, private tennis courts, and four-star golf courses. He drives a hulking SUV and travels to his mountain home at least once a month. The label on his suits is Armani. He smokes Cuban cigars and drinks imported Scottish whiskey. He has platinum in his wallet, diversity in his portfolio, and blue in his blood. He wants for nothing and has everything. He has so much that Lazarus just wants the scraps of bread that are cast away from his table.

William Barclay tells us that in that day, there were no napkins and few utensils. The wealthy would use large hunks of bread to wipe their hands or blot the corners of their mouths. They would then pitch these improvised napkins away from the table to be thrown out with the garbage.[4] Lazarus wants these scraps—the garbage—to fill his growling stomach, but even this Rich Man's garbage is too good for Lazarus. Even his dumpster is locked behind closed gates.

Jesus again attacks the calloused attitude of the religious-social-political leaders of his nation. Many of these more successful types had adopted the attitude that they were successful because God was on their side, or the side of their nation. The prevailing attitude among the Pharisees and experts of the religious law was that all of Israel would be saved, but not necessarily the sinners and outcasts. The identity of these sinners and outcasts was obvious. They were the ones whom God had set his hand against and who had forfeited any opportunity at redemption.

"I have what I have because God favors me. But he doesn't favor you. Why? Well, you are obviously a sinner. How else can your beggary be explained? You are sick and helpless, in poverty and shame, thus confirming your sin. Off to hell with you so the kingdom will come."

While this is a Jewish context, it is not unique. Many Christians live with this same conclusion today. There is nothing wrong with acknowledging that God has blessed us; that is proper and right. But to say that God favors us over those who have less, or those who have suffered, or those who have had serious illness or hardship, or those born in a developing country on a continent far away, or those with a different color skin or of another race is to put ourselves in danger of judgment's fire.

Seeing those in need is not an opportunity to analyze, condemn, and judge. It is an opportunity to show compassion and justice, to unleash God's grace on the world. The Good Samaritan, the Great Banquet, the Prodigal Son—all these stories keep stacking up and circling back to the same place: it is easy to judge sinners we think unworthy of entrance into the kingdom of God, but God's mercy overcomes human unworthiness. The refusal to offer this same kind of heavenly mercy and instead remain in self-centered arrogance trips the do-gooders and lands them outside the kingdom themselves.

So the story of Lazarus and the Rich Man sets the stage for Jesus once again to turn the tables on religion, and this time with yet another creative twist. This is the reason, I think, that the beggar in our story is named. He is a nobody. Disposable. Expendable. A worthless sinner obviously living under God's judgment, the Pharisees would say. But Jesus says, "Not so fast. He has a name. He is Lazarus. He is somebody in God's eyes."

Heightening the contrast, the Rich Man is without a name. While everyone seeks to shake his hand, recruit him for their fundraising campaigns, ask him to sit on their advisory board, and get him on their party list, he is the true nobody in this story.

The contrast between these two continues even at death. Lazarus dies and remains unburied. The Jewish people believed that not getting a proper burial was a certain sign of God's judgment.[5] It is likely that his body was dragged to the community's landfill. Unceremoniously, and just as in life, his corpse is cast aside as garbage, and he finds his final resting place alongside those scraps of bread he wanted to eat, consumed by maggots, the previously mentioned starving dogs, and the flames.

The Rich Man, however, is "buried." He probably got a weeklong funeral. Several ministers and long-time friends delivered the eulogy. Members of the Rotary Club served as honorary pallbearers. He received a full-page obituary in the newspaper, and a park on the outskirts of town was named in his honor.

Then Jesus rapidly moves the action to the afterlife. The angels carry Lazarus to Abraham's side. However, the Rich Man, as the old King James English says, "lifts up his eyes in hell." But the King James Version is wrong.

The Bible uses four different words often rendered "hell" in our English translations. One is used in the Old Testament and the other three in the New Testament. The single Hebrew word of the Old Testament is *sheol*. Literally, it means the "unseen." Thirty-one times the King James Version translates *sheol* as "hell." Thirty-one times it is rendered "the grave," and three times *sheol* is translated "the pit." The most accurate of these is simply "the grave" or the "place of the dead."

The afterlife, an actual hell, and even the resurrection are undeveloped concepts and more than a bit vague in the Jewish thought of the Old Testament period. Many of the ideas about the afterlife that we associate with Judeo-Christian theology were not introduced until the decades leading up to the first century AD, and many of those ideas are from the Greeks, Persians, and Babylonians, not the Jews.

The Pharisees, Jesus' old antagonists, interestingly enough, were the ones who brought hell and heaven into the Jewish mainstream. See, something had to be done for the good and righteous, like the heroes of the past, the heroes of their wars for independence. They could not simply be left as dust in the ground. There had to be vindication. They, meaning the righteous and pious ones, would be resurrected.[6] The sinners, lawbreakers, tax collectors, the Gentiles and Samaritans, the beggars and outcasts—well, they would go to hell, or what the New Testament calls *hades* in the Greek, the word Jesus uses here in Luke 16.

Hades is the New Testament equivalent of *sheol.* It is "the grave" or "the place of the dead," used eleven times in the New Testament. In the Jewish thinking of the day, *Hades* was in sight of Paradise, or Abraham's Bosom, that intermediate place where the saints of old and the faithful dead awaited resurrection, just as in Jesus' story here.[7] The suffering ones, those who had been disobedient to the pious ways of God, were in *Hades,* and they could see the good people enjoying themselves on the other side. This served to intensify their sufferings.

The religious leaders of Jesus' day held the fires of judgment over the heads of marginalized sinners as a way of reform: "Straighten up or God is going to get you." Thus, the Pharisees and their ilk became the authoritative keepers of the door, judging who passed and who failed, who got in and who was left out. Now, it is impossible to say how much of this is strictly Jewish thought and how much is borrowed from other cultures, like the Persians and the Greeks, but these were the conclusions of the religious leaders of Jesus' day, and it was all convenient.[8]

Hades, then, is not "hell" as we have understood it or as I saw it portrayed on the silver screen at Glade Baptist Church so many years ago. *Hades* is the grave, the underworld, the unseen place where the souls of the dead go.

Moving on to more hellish vocabulary, the most often translated word for "hell" in the New Testament is the word *gehenna.* Though used in the New Testament, it is a Hebrew word referring to a specific place, here in this world, not necessarily the world to come. *Gehenna* was and is the deep, narrow Valley of Ge Hinnom south of Jerusalem. There, the Palestinian ancients worshiped their fire gods, and the idolatrous Jews of the kingdom period sacrificed their children to Molech. Because of its distasteful past, it eventually became a landfill, the city dump, where the trash and refuse of Jerusalem was cast. After the Babylonians destroyed Jerusalem in 586 BC, it was filled almost to capacity with the bodies of starved and slaughtered Israelites. In Jesus' day the bodies of criminals, rejects, and the poor who were without burial sites—like our friend Lazarus—were cast there to rot in the open air. For generations on end, *gehenna* represented everything filthy, rejected, and under judgment.

We are hard pressed then, to make hell (read *gehenna*), as we have so often accepted it, anything different than the city of Jerusalem's landfill, for that is how Jesus used the word. In fact, of the dozen times the word *gehenna* is used in the New Testament, Jesus uses that word exclusively in all of them except for one.[9] No one else in the entire canon of Scripture, Old or New Testament, uses the word.

Listening to American preaching for the last couple of hundred years, one would think the eternal burning hell was on every page in the Bible, but it is not. And when the term is used in the Bible, it is a direct reference to a specific place known by the residents of Jerusalem. The Rich Man is not in an eternal blazing *gehenna*, or *The Burning Hell* of Estus Pirkle's imagination. He is in the place of the dead, *hades* or *sheol.* This does not mean he is pleased with the arrangement, for he is still in a bad place and obviously under judgment.

Why is he there? What crime is he paying for? Those who want to make this parable specifically about heaven and hell have a problem here. The only reason implied by Jesus that lands the Rich Man in the flames is his wealth. Likewise, the only reason Lazarus is in paradise is because he was poor. If we follow this literal line of thought, as many commentators do, then we should all become beggars, acquire sores on our bodies, and go down to the pound and let a few rabid dogs chew on our ankles, and then when we die we'll get to go to heaven. Those of us with resources, with an expensive automobile, a nice house, and a savings account, well, because we possess these things, it means we are going to *hades* in a hand basket. Obviously, this is not Jesus' point.

So what is the point?

On this Great Journey, the Pharisees and the experts in the religious law have kept their rules at the expense of the suffering of those around them. They have turned religion into a poison that hurts people rather than helps them. They have tried more to manipulate the masses than set people free. They have cuddled up with the Roman Empire to keep and consolidate their power, they have complained and muttered over Jesus inviting the marginalized into the coming kingdom, and they have ignored God's personal invitation to join the family in celebration.

Here Jesus is not teaching about the specifics of heaven, hell, *hades, gehenna,* purgatory, or paradise. He is saying, "The ones you think are going to hell aren't going there at all. They are actually children of Abraham, who regardless of their prodigal, sinful, misfortunate appearance will be welcomed to the table. It is you, who think of yourselves as rich, safe, protected and untouchable, with your flowing robes of purple and great feasts, who will be cast into judgment."

Jesus is turning the "hell-fire" language of judgment against the very inventers, adapters, and users of the language. Just as the initially invited guests found themselves outside the Great Banquet, those who think their religion, status, and rule keeping will save them from judgment have another thought coming. We cannot consign to hell all the people we think are unacceptable to God. These may be the ones sitting at heaven's feast, the true children of God, while the rule-keeping moralists look on at a miserable distance.

The native peoples of what is now Canada and Alaska tell of the effective but grisly way that their ancestors rid themselves of wolves that preyed on their villages. A hunter dipped a sharpened knife in seal blood and allowed it to freeze in the Arctic air. He repeated the process many times, with the layers of blood freezing and thickening, until he had what looked like a crimson popsicle. One evening the hunter stuck the knife point-up in the snow. The wolf was drawn to the smell of this bloody treat, and upon finding it he begin to lick it ravenously. The wolf's craving for blood was so instinctively strong that the animal did not realize the blade eventually cut his own mouth. The more he attacked the knife, the faster he died, feasting on his own blood. By morning the wolf was dead.

As the church, we must be terribly careful whom we threaten with hell's fire. When we act without compassion and grace, when we harshly and judgmentally begin to determine by our own opinion who is in and who is out, when we attempt to lock others out—we actually put ourselves out. We risk coming under the same judgment under which we place others. The souls we kill are our own, hemorrhaged away by an insatiable thirst for seeing others come under judgment.

But before we take to the road again with Jesus, leaving this parable behind, we should stop and listen to Abraham's words to the Rich Man in verse 31. The Rich Man, now in judgment, is concerned for his brothers who still live. He appeals for Lazarus to be sent to them to warn them.

Speaking of the Rich Man's brothers, Abraham says, "If they won't listen to Moses and the prophets, they won't listen even if someone rises from the dead."

The Pharisees' belief system, like many of our own, was like a closed window. When a window is always open, it is not a window. It is a hole in the wall. The cold, the heat, the dust and dirt can all blow in and ruin what is inside, or at least make things uncomfortable. If you close a window and never open it, however, then it becomes nothing but a wall. You can't get a fresh breath of air. You can't crack it just to get a smell of the fresh outdoors. And you certainly can't speak to someone on the other side. A constantly closed window is useless.

The Pharisees and experts in the religious law had a closed window when it came to the things they believed. It was painted and nailed shut. Thus, they could not grasp Jesus' audacious message. It was too far outside their frame of view. It did not match the answers about everything of which they were already convinced: window closed, case closed, hearts closed.

Not even a resurrection itself—do not miss the irony of Jesus' words—would be enough to let fresh air blow across their dusty, mold-infested conclusions. Jesus saw the Pharisees and experts in the religious law, who were the professional Bible interpreters, as not even recognizing what the Bible was really about.

They didn't get it. They were blind to true spirituality, which is to "do justice, love mercy, and walk humbly with God" (Mic 6:8). They misinterpreted the whole of the holy text, making it an encyclopedic rulebook that was impossible to lift rather than the living, breathing guide stone by which we are formed into lovers of God and of our neighbors. They replaced the simple, compassionate ways of reflecting God's true nature with a hideous form of legalism that inflated the egos of its leaders and crushed the spirits of the seekers.

A few chapters ago, we catalogued the commandments of the Old Testament. Again, the Torah contains 613 individual commandments. 365 of those are negative: "Thou shalt not." 248 are positive: "Thou shalt." These dos and do nots were the focus of the religious leaders. Yet here is what they missed: more than 2,000 passages reveal God's compassion for the poor, the widows, the orphans, the refugees, and the outsiders who are suffering injustice.

God's prevailing command to his people, those who have received his grace, is not to glory in their position—"I've got mine; don't you wish you did too." No, our vocation is to be extenders of grace to those who have yet to receive it. Being the people of God is not a position of privilege, like a rich man locked behind his security fence. It is a task to do mission, to care for the Lazaruses of the world.

We in the revivalist tradition have viewed grace only in terms of privatized, individualized spirituality. Give people enough Jesus to save their souls, move them to an emotional decision, help them get their hearts right and acquire a more responsible morality, and that will be enough. But that is *not* enough. It is not even the beginning of enough. God was concerned about those living in dire suffering long before Bono, Angelina Jolie, or George Clooney turned into social activists.

Professed followers of Christ will have no credibility in this suffering world full of Lazaruses if we remain in our temples, sanctuaries, and gated communities keeping the rules, counting our money, and looking down on others with condescension. Jesus says to us, loud and clear: "Your mistreatment of those on the outside of your religious system will land you in the fires of judgment."

So what are we to do? How are we to live?

We must take note of Jesus' confrontations with the religious on his journey to Jerusalem. Then we must follow him as the true and living way. Jesus is an open path—much more open than many of us are ready to accept. Jesus has not padlocked himself in, hiding behind a steel and concrete door, waiting for those with just the right code to get through.

His arms are open. His way is open. His heart is open. And he says to all who will, "Come to me and find out who God really is. Come to me and find truth. Come to me and you will find out what life is all about. Come to me and you will find all the grace and love you need, enough to give to the people around you, as I have given it to you."

Allow me a question, oddly enough, asked of the congregation that watched *The Burning Hell* in those north Georgia hills: Will you follow Jesus?

Not as the means of escaping hell and getting to heaven; that is not even the point of this parable, and not the point of most of Jesus' teaching, preaching, and storytelling. Instead, will you follow him as the way to know God and enter the kingdom of heaven, that daring, earth-shattering way of life meant to revolutionize the world today?

For today is the day of salvation, and the kingdom of God is at hand.

Notes

1. Connie Post, personal e-mail to author, 6 June 1999.

2. *The Burning Hell*, dir. Ron Ormond, written by Ron Ormond and Estus Pirkle, 1974.

3. Leon Morris, *Luke*, rev. ed., Tyndale New Testament Commentaries (Grand Rapids: Eerdmans, 1995), 275.

4. William Barclay, *The Parables of Jesus* (Louisville: Westminster John Knox, 1999), 93.

5. George Arthur Buttrick and S. MacLean Gilmour, *The Interpreter's Bible*, vol. 8 (Nashville: Abingdon Press, 1987), 291.

6. Ibid., 290.

7. The Jews seem to have adapted a distinct Greek idea here, with *hades* and *tartarus* both being at the end of the River Styx, but in sight of each other. See Kenneth Wuest, *Treasures from the Greek New Testament* (Grand Rapids: Eerdmans, 1969), 44–45.

8. Barclay, *Parables of Jesus*, 94.

9. James 3:6.

Reflection Questions

1. Do you think hell is used as a threat to correct people, to keep them in line? How have you experienced its use?

2. How prevalent is the idea that "good" people prosper and those less so suffer setbacks, poverty, and the like? Is this an accurate belief to which to hold?

3. In this chapter I say that Jesus was turning the "hell-fire language of judgment" against those who used it for their own purposes. Why do you agree or disagree?

4. Why do the thousands of verses in the Bible about justice and mercy for the poor, widowed, and orphaned not get more attention?

5. Is Jesus more open than most of us are willing to acknowledge? Explain your answer.

____

____

____

____

____

Chapter 14

I Came Back, One Last Time, to Say "Thank You"

> You have some amongst you to whom you could do good. See that you do not fail them.
>
> —The Epistle of Barnabas

His name is George Mayo Livingston III. His grandmother gave him the nickname "Buz" as a child and it stuck. I'm glad. I know Buz and could not think of calling him George, Mayo, or something else that sounds like a sandwich condiment.

Buz and I are friends, neighbors, and fellow patriots in the Georgia Bulldog nation. He is as rabid a fan as I have ever met. Buz is also a financial adviser, a suitable but unforeseen vocation. After college graduation, Buz returned home to the peanuts and row crops of the family's South Georgia farm, but the farming life could not hold him. Instead, he bought a local business, put his kids through school, and after his children left home, he and his wife uprooted themselves and moved to the beach. He became a certified financial planner, and he is pretty darn good at it too.

But Buz and I share more than an affection for Bulldog football and our native Georgia soil. We both love a good story, and we have swapped more than a few tall tales in the last several years. Buz sent me this story recently from the world of finance, knowing I would love it. I share it here with you because it is too good to keep to myself:

> It's the story of Marilyn Mock. You wouldn't know her. She's not running for president. She is 50 years old and has a rock yard business in Texas, which she runs with her three kids. Last weekend, she went to a foreclosure auction with her son to see him bid on a house. While he was signing the papers, she wandered back to the auction area and sat down on the floor next to a woman named Tracy Orr. Being friendly, Mock asked if Orr was bidding on a house.

No answer.

She asked again.

Orr started crying.

Then she opened the brochure and pointed. "That's my house," she told Mock.

The truth was, that had been her house. Orr paid $80,000 for it four years ago. Then, like a lot of Americans, she lost her job and wasn't able to keep up with the payments. Eventually, the bank foreclosed. Orr, who is now a housekeeper, had come to the auction as a way to say good-bye. Mock listened to her story. Saw her tears. And before she knew what she was doing, she was raising her hand as the property was on the block.

"I had no idea what this house was," Mock later told me. "I didn't even know where the town was!"

But she kept bidding. And at $30,000, it was hers. She turned to the sobbing Orr and said, "I did this for you."

Can you believe that? Mock plunked down 30 grand for a total stranger, with no idea if the woman could pay her back.

"I just know she went from complete sadness to complete happiness," Mock said. "And it really makes you happy when you can do something for somebody."

The two women have since worked out a deal. Mock—who is hardly wealthy—took a loan out against her dump truck to buy the house. And Orr plans to make those payments each month, thus slowly paying it off. Meanwhile, Orr gets to live in her home again. And both women now have a new best friend.

"I've got somebody that, if I ever get depressed or something," Mock said, laughing, "I can call and gripe and I think she'll probably understand."

Now, remember, there was nothing in this for Mock. The attention she has gotten all came after the fact. Her son, Dustin, told me that he was not surprised, that she always had been this way—the type of person who would see a struggling mother in line at the supermarket and pay for her groceries, no questions asked.

"I shake my head at her," Dustin Mock said, "but she's always done good things, for me and everybody else. It's a body of work, to be honest."

Mock was asked that day: Why did you do it? Why come to the rescue of a stranger?

"She needed help," was the answer.[1]

Jesus encountered a group of ten strangers, living and suffering together, with little to be thankful for. So Jesus went to work. Why? Because they simply needed help. The account found in Luke 17:11-19 tells of ten men suffering from leprosy:

> As Jesus continued on toward Jerusalem, he reached the border between Galilee and Samaria. As he entered a village there, ten lepers stood at a distance, crying out, "Jesus, Master, have mercy on us!"
>
> He looked at them and said, "Go show yourselves to the priests." And as they went, they were cleansed of their leprosy.
>
> One of them, when he saw that he was healed, came back to Jesus, shouting, "Praise God!" He fell to the ground at Jesus' feet, thanking him for what he had done. This man was a Samaritan.
>
> Jesus asked, "Didn't I heal ten men? Where are the other nine? Has no one returned to give glory to God except this foreigner?" And Jesus said to the man, "Stand up and go. Your faith has healed you."

These ten men are lepers—not big cats with spots—but lepers. That is, these men suffer from leprosy. From a distance, the group shouts to Jesus, asking for his help. They do not ask for healing directly, only for mercy. But certainly healing is what they want, to be made well, to be restored.

How they found out about Jesus, being isolated from society, we do not know. Maybe they stayed on the edges of the massive crowds following him to Jerusalem. Even here they were careful to keep their distance and make their request by shouting across the countryside to Jesus. This group followed established social protocol. Leprosy was highly contagious and had to be controlled. Those with the disease were quarantined into colonies. Those unfortunate enough to contract the disease were thus cut off from family and friends, from the practice of faith, and from involvement in the community, typically for the rest of their lives.

Luke places this episode within the Great Journey of Jesus, bringing into focus the ultimate collection of outsiders: lepers who were legally, socially, and religiously cut off not just from the synagogue, but from Jewish life altogether.

It is hard for us to imagine the stigma attached to this disease, as we do not encounter those with leprosy—not here in the West, anyway. Leprosy, known today as Hansen's Disease, is a bacterial ailment that affects the nerve endings in human skin. There are only about a million cases of the disease in the world today, and with about $200 worth of antibiotics and treatment, it can be completely cured. But in Jesus' day it was a death sentence.

Degenerating and disfiguring, leprosy devastated the skin, the eyes, and the respiratory tract of the sufferer. Slowly the nerve endings began to lose sensation. There was no way to feel anything. Then the skin turned a milky white and became gangrenous. Those suffering from advanced stages of the disease lost fingers, toes, noses, whole feet and hands. If the extremities were not lost, they were often damaged and deformed by the disease. It was possible to live, or at least exist like this, anywhere from two to forty years.

In past centuries, Christian organizations have done more to eradicate this disease than anyone else, based largely on the compassion with which Christ responded to lepers. He was never afraid to minister to them, to touch them, and to embrace them.

One such pioneer was a United Methodist missionary named Mary Reed. In the late 1800s and early 1900s, Reed was one of the first to live among those with leprosy. In time she acquired the disease herself, was forced to abandon her family, and went to live in the Indian Himalayas with the sufferers of the Chandag leper colony. There she organized and led a little church, cared for the sick and dying for thirty years, and then died herself. Largely forgotten today, she was once regarded as "one of the loneliest, yet one of the most noble women in the world." Mary Reed, caring for less than a hundred of the quarter million Indian lepers, pried open the door for literally millions to find physical and spiritual healing.[2]

Without a doubt, the modern-day equivalent of leprosy in the West has been the HIV/AIDS epidemic. Just as many of the religious leaders of Jesus' day saw leprosy as a judgment of God, all too many view AIDS sufferers today in the same light. To the detriment of those suffering with the disease, we get stuck on who has it and how the virus is transferred.

Today more than a million Americans carry HIV, but more than thirty million people carry the virus worldwide, with a staggering seventy-five percent of all cases found in sub-Sahara Africa. There are now twelve million AIDS-created African orphans.[3] Christians can and should respond to this kind of suffering, not with pulpit pounding and picket sign rants, but with human touch, compassionate truth, and the Spirit of Christ. We must overcome our stigmas, our fears, and our compassion fatigue to embrace those who are suffering, just as Jesus did. For that was Jesus' mission: spiritual and physical healing that included those kept on the outside.

Jimmy Allen is a former Southern Baptist Convention president and pastor, most recently serving as pastor of the nondenominational chapel at Big Canoe in the North Georgia Mountains. Jimmy's daughter-in-law,

Lydia, contracted HIV from a blood transfusion just hours before her first son was born. The virus went undetected until Lydia and Scott Allen, Jimmy's son, had a second child, Bryan. Bryan died of AIDS as an infant in 1986. Lydia's death followed in 1992.

Meanwhile, Jimmy Allen's other adult child revealed that he was gay, and he too was HIV positive. At the time when all of this was tearing the family apart, Scott Allen was a young associate minister at a church in Colorado Springs, Colorado. His wife was dying, his children were HIV positive, and his brother was out of the closet. He went to his boss, the senior pastor of the church, and confided in him their struggles. The following day Scott was fired. When the family moved to the Dallas-Ft. Worth area, no church of any denomination would accept their son Matthew in Sunday school. They were quite literally thrown out on the street.

In recent years, Scott Allen has forsaken Christianity altogether. Scott, deeply wounded, says, "It's just a business like any other business. Churches do what pleases the most customers." His conclusion is that the church wants the most undesirable of our society to just go away.

"Our churches are big on calling people to repent," says Jimmy Allen. "Now it's time for the church to repent for rejecting people who are hurt and in need."[4]

Jesus rejects no one—not sufferers of AIDS, not sufferers of leprosy. We should act no different than the one we call Lord.

Jesus tells these lepers, "Go show yourselves to the priests" (v. 14).

Why did Jesus give this strange kind of instruction? The process established by Jewish law was such that if one became a leper, he or she had to go into seclusion. That much has been established. There was, however, an avenue by which to reenter society. If by chance the leper got well, if by some miracle of God health was restored, the leper went to visit the local priest.

In an elaborate ceremony, the priest examined the skin. If he found no evidence of the disease, he killed a few birds and released one into the wild, threw back some olive oil, and jumped up and down on his right foot while patting his head and rubbing his belly (I'm exaggerating a little here). Then the former leper was allowed to go home to friends and family. Reentry into the community was approved as the once suffering leper received a certified document pronouncing him or her clean. You can read more about this in Leviticus 14:2-32.

This practice has been explained in such a way as to make the temple priest a kind of doctor. I do not think that is the case. This is not a medical examination. The priest performs the restoration ceremony because it is a theological ceremony. Those with leprosy were unclean, like Samaritans, tax collectors, adulterers, and other sinners. God's hand of judgment was heavy upon them. The people believed that is why they suffered. For a leper to awaken with sudden spotless skin was surely a sign of repentance and a turning to God. This is why the priest was involved. He was the gatekeeper, making sure the wrong crowd did not get through the door and back into the community. Still, not yet healing them, Jesus sends them to get their certification papers of a clean bill of health from the priest.

"And as they went," Luke tells us, "they were cleansed of their leprosy."

Mercifully, Jesus heals these poor souls. Maybe fingers began to grow back into place. Fully inflatable lungs replaced difficult breathing. White, splotchy skin and hunks of black flesh became as pink and healthy as a baby's bottom. For the first time in years, they were physically well.

This group of ten turns together from death's door, but they do not turn together toward their healer. Only one of the ten, overwhelmed by what just happened, comes back to Jesus. He falls at Jesus' feet and worships.

Outside of other crusty lepers, Jesus is the first person this man would have gotten close to in years. He did not continue on to the temple to see the priest or run home to the wife he had not held in his arms for so long. He did not go immediately to scoop up the children he had only seen play at a distance on the other side of a chain-link fence, or run to his aging parents to kiss them a final time. No, he went first and foremost to Jesus and threw himself on the ground before him in complete submission.

This is a thankful man, a grateful man who knows he is a recipient of grace. The tragedy is that he was the only one who returned to say, "Thank you." Even Jesus was surprised. "Didn't I heal ten men?" Jesus asks rhetorically. "Then where are the other nine?"

Just when we think we finally have a story without innuendo and the biting wit we have come to appreciate in Jesus, he whacks us once again with the punch line: "Has no one returned to give glory to God except this foreigner?"

This grateful, worshiping man at the feet of a Jewish rabbi is a Samaritan: a foreigner, an illegal alien, an outsider. I will not replay for you the Parable of the Good Samaritan from an earlier chapter. I will remind you, however, that Samaritans and Jews were bitter racial, cultural, and religious enemies. They hated one another, each sentencing the other to destruction outside the kingdom of God. Yet here, this foreigner, this outsider from the lowest caste of Jewish society, was thankful. An exile who bore the shame of his disease, his nationality, and his religion, this stranger understood better and responded more appropriately to grace than all the others.

Jesus is not putting the man down by bringing up his ethnicity. He is highlighting once again that even the outlander can put his faith in the right place. Even the ultimate oddball, unworthy and untouchable, is welcome at the feet of Christ and in the arms of God.

This story ends with Jesus saying to the now-made-well Samaritan, "Stand up and go. Your faith has healed you."

Pause a moment over these words. Do you want to travel this road with Jesus? Then recognize that the only reason you travel with him is that he has invited you along. In the words of Brennan Manning, "We are all beggars at the door of God's mercy!"[5] Yet he takes us beggars along for the ride. We go with him to love and serve our neighbors; to resist the manipulation and coercion of religious systems that enslave rather than free; to surrender our agendas on how we think the world ought to be run; to rejoice when an outsider stumbles her way to the table of God and a prodigal son staggers back into the Father's house; to recognize that the true children of God and residents of the kingdom are not the high and mighty who have their act together. They are those who have received an undeserved, unearned, unadulterated grace, and our only response is to fall on our faces before Jesus and say, "Thank you."

In turn he says to us, "Now stand up and go. Go be the light of the world. Go be the salt of the earth. Go be conduits of my mercy and goodness. As you have received grace, grant it to others. As you have been forgiven, forgive others. Your faith has made you well. Give that healing faith to the suffering and the sinners and the marginalized and the outsiders around you; for these too can enter the kingdom of God by the same grace you have received. Stand up and go."

We cannot remain at the feet of Jesus, shooing away anyone else who would come to worship him. It is not our responsibility to protect Jesus' image by screening those who arrive, dry and thirsty, looking for a sip of his mercy. Followers of Jesus do not sit guard. They go, multiplying the grace they have received all along the way.

Georgia mountain farmer Grethel Thomas was part of the church I once pastored. His wife and daughter actually attended church. Grethel stayed out on the edge. We saw him on occasion, but not much. He was much more comfortable on Sunday mornings with his cows or in the hay field.

Grethel was killed in a farming accident on December 24, 1997. Even though it was a holiday, cows still had to be fed, and he was moving hay out to the fields. Since it was foggy and wet, he failed to see oncoming traffic and pulled his tractor out in front of a car as he crossed the highway. He was struck and killed immediately. As you might imagine, his family was devastated, not the least of which was his only child, a teenage daughter named Greta, the child of his old age.

Greta called me right away, and I went to her family's home on an awful Christmas Eve. A few days later we had the funeral. I had a small part in the service, as an old Baptist preacher I had never met, T. J. Cleveland, gave the main eulogy.

T. J. came into the funeral home on crutches, limping and moving slowly. I didn't think much about it. He was elderly. He toddled up to the pulpit when it was his time to speak, alternating between holding on to the podium and his crutches. With tears rolling off his face, he began his eulogy by saying, "I came back today, one last time, to say 'thank you.'" T. J. then told this story.

In the summer of 1944, Grethel and T. J. were young men who found themselves in the 361st Regimental Combat Team of the 91st Infantry Division of the U.S. Army, making landings in Italy. Their unit engaged the German and Italian enemy in what is now called the Gothic Line Campaign. These were dreadful days of heat, fear, bloodshed, and loss. The campaign consisted of bitter fighting pillbox to pillbox, foxhole to foxhole, weaving through barbed wire entanglements and negotiating mine fields.

T. J. stepped on one of these mines. It blew off his legs and propelled him off a steep ridge to a valley below. It was the heat of battle. With bullets still flying, T. J. called out to his friends to leave him to die. Grethel refused. Taking most of a day, and bearing shrapnel in his own body from the blast, Grethel zigzagged his way through the mine field, ducked ricocheting bullets, and rappelled into the ravine to where his friend lay dying. Grethel carried T. J. out of the valley, back through the minefield, and up the ridge to safety. Unknown to many of us in his church and community, Grethel was a decorated hero, recipient of the Bronze Star and the Purple Heart.

T. J., an old man in 1997, had been given back his life by this friend, this hero he now honored.

"I came back, one last time, to say 'thank you.'"[6]

"Has no one returned to give glory to God except this foreigner?"

One did come back to say "thank you," and Jesus told him, "Now, stand up and go."

Go live.

Go breathe deeply the rich grace of God.

Go share this goodness with others.

Go with Jesus wherever this journey leads.

Notes

1. As told by Mitch Albom, *The Mitch Album Show,* WJR-AM 760, 2 November 2008.

2. *New York Times,* "American Woman Aids Indian Lepers," Special Cable, 13 April 1921.

3. Statistics available at AVERT, online at http://www.avert.org/statindx.htm (accessed 1 March 2008).

4. Terry Mattingly, "Jimmy Allen, the Church and AIDS," online article, http://www.tmatt.net/1995/11/29/jimmy-allen-the-church-and-aids/, (accessed 29 February 2008).

5. Brennan Manning, *The Ragamuffin Gospel* (Colorado Springs: Multnomah Publishers, 2005), 26.

6. Story used by permission from Greta Thomas, in personal e-mail to the author, 11 December 2006. Grethel Thomas's partner in T. J. Cleveland's rescue was Clarence Harrison, also decorated for his heroics.

Reflection Questions

1. What groups or individuals are ostracized today as lepers were in Jesus' day? Why is this? How should the church respond to these individuals and groups?

2. Why did the nine other lepers healed by Jesus not return to thank him?

3. How, specifically and practically, can the grace you have received overflow into the lives of others?

4. This account reveals a dual temptation: living without gratitude on the one hand, or sitting at the feet of Jesus, thankful but withdrawn on the other. How do we avoid these two pitfalls?

5. Read again this quote from Scott Allen: "It's just a business like any other business. Churches do what pleases the most customers." Do you agree or disagree?

_____

_____

_____

_____

_____

Chapter 15

Kyrie Eliason

> Religion is an abyss; it is terror. Death is the meaning of religion.
>
> —Karl Barth

> Then Jesus told this story to some who had great confidence in their own righteousness and scorned everyone else: "Two men went to the temple to pray. One was a Pharisee, and the other was a despised tax collector. The Pharisee stood by himself and prayed this prayer: 'I thank you, God, that I am not a sinner like everyone else. For I don't cheat, I don't sin, and I don't commit adultery. I'm certainly not like that tax collector! I fast twice a week, and I give you a tenth of my income.'
>
> "But the tax collector stood at a distance and dared not even lift his eyes to heaven as he prayed. Instead, he beat his chest in sorrow, saying, 'O God, be merciful to me, for I am a sinner.' I tell you, this sinner, not the Pharisee, returned home justified before God. For those who exalt themselves will be humbled, and those who humble themselves will be exalted." (Luke 18:9-14)

The above parable is Jesus' coup de grace, the final push toward the finish line of this Great Journey in Luke. Appropriately enough, the setting for this tale is the Jewish temple where Luke's narrative has taken Jesus all along, and us with him. In the temple, two familiar men are praying: a Pharisee and a tax collector.

There is nothing new here. Not really. Jesus is beating the same drum, singing another verse of the same song, calling us past the smugness and self-righteousness of religion to a life of complete dependence on his grace.

My engineering friend Walt Horne would call this journey, with its repetitive lessons, "creep." I thought creep was a person, someone disgusting or sleazy; the slimeball across the room that you know you should avoid. Or maybe creep was something you did. To creep is to crawl slowly along the ground, sneaking up on someone. Walt, with his Georgia Tech education for which I have forgiven him, gave me a different definition altogether.

Creep is a deformation that occurs in metals over a period of time when the material is subjected to constant stress at constant temperature. Not to get overly technical, but if you want to bend a metal, you use a temperature and pressure that is below the metal's threshold, below its ultimate strength. In other words, the metal can bear it. It can withstand it, because the goal is not to break or destroy the metal, but to shape it.

Over time the temperature and pressure wear down the molecular structure and the metal begins to move. It can be shaped into whatever the engineer wants. After shaping the material, the engineer removes the heat and the pressure, and he or she is left with girders for a bridge, fence posts for the farm, cola cans, or whatever the engineer wants. Again, the goal is not to pulverize the metal like a blacksmith. The goal is to bend it slowly, with constant pressure.

The calling of Christ, the call to follow him away from the religious, social, and emotional illusions of security we have known, is a "creeping" process. He keeps these nagging but generally tolerable questions in our mind about how we should respond to others. He keeps bringing across our path people we do not particularly care for or want to be around and using them to shape us. He slams us against our own preconceptions and judgments, and remarkably, over time he wears down our old ways of thinking, and we find ourselves moving. Creep, creep, creep, pressure and heat, stress and temperature: Christ bends, shapes, and engineers his followers into what he wants us to be.

Inside this stumbling, bumbling body known as the church—inside each of us—with our failures, shortcomings, and inherent fallenness—is the crucified, but resurrected, living, breathing Christ. He has chosen to love you, indwell you, and cause you to be his love in the world. You. He has no "Plan B." You—we—are it. Out of these malfunctioning hands, feet, and mouth he speaks and moves. The movement and message is one of received grace and therefore shared grace with all who cross our paths, especially those we find most difficult to love—for those are the ones who need it most. Like tax collectors and Pharisees.

Several years ago, on the courthouse steps of the town in which I lived, there was a rally. It was not a gathering like the Ku Klux Klan had when I was a teenager, but it was close. A homosexual couple in our community was seeking to become foster parents. You can imagine the kickback that erupted in a small Southern town. But it wasn't just the members of our community who were most vocal in protest. Gathered on the courthouse steps of our fair city were representatives of a religious group from Washington D.C. and points beyond, present to speak out in holy fury. This group came down to help us uphold our moral standards.

At the time, my office was downtown. I strolled up the street to check it out, and what I found was horrifying. Lacing their speeches with Scripture readings from the King James Bible, shaking the recognizable "God Hates Fags" signs, preacher after preacher raged with some of the most vicious and hateful words I have ever heard. I could not believe how angry and poisonous it was.

One of the police officers watching over the proceedings walked up and asked me, "What do think about this, preacher?"

I knew this officer. He was a good, keep-your-nose-clean, redneck kid. But he was not a follower of Christ. Obviously he knew me as a member of the clergy. So I turned it back on him and asked, "What do you think?"

He answered, "This is why you all ought to keep your church and Bible to yourself."

Dorothy Sayers was fond of saying that Jesus endured three great humiliations in his redemption of humankind: the incarnation, the cross, and the church.[1] Jesus, the Christ, the head, mind, and intelligence of the new creation, is trapped inside a spastic, debilitated, malfunctioning body—a body called the church. Rather than communicating clearly the love and grace of God, we obscure and twist the message so that it cannot be heard correctly. More often than we care to admit, it comes across as hateful news, not good news. We who have drunk freely from the cup of grace respond to others with anything but grace.

That is what I felt most when I stood near the courthouse steps on that Friday afternoon. These people, exercising their freedom of speech for which I am so thankful for, and would go to the wall for, attached hateful words and spiteful talk to the name of God. Somehow, in the convulsive twisting of the body of Christ, the message also got twisted. I felt ashamed just standing there.

The following Sunday I fumed from my own church pulpit about how we are called to love our neighbors as ourselves—even the people we just know God condemns. Loving your neighbor goes beyond feeding their dog or keeping an eye on their home while they are out of town. No, to love our neighbor as we love ourselves, I rightfully said that Sunday, is to love whoever we meet, whoever is in need, no matter who they are.

If they live across the street or on another continent; if they are black or white; if they are straight or gay; if they are Latino or Anglo; if they are of my political persuasion or not; if they are Christian or Muslim; if they are my buddy on the bar stool beside me or someone I would never shake hands with, they are my neighbor. As a follower of Christ, my responsibility extends to them to love them—without prejudice or bias.

Oh, my sermon was good; it was a holy tirade. But over the course of the next few days, the next few weeks, my "good feelings" ebbed away and conviction replaced them. What made me feel so good, and what brought what I can only describe as God's heavy "creeping" hand down on my heart, was this: it made me feel good to hate the people who were being hateful and to do it in the name of loving others, to do it in the name of Christ.

My "loving" words were nothing more than a variation of the words and behavior I condemned. Street preachers railed against and hated homosexuals, abortionists, teenagers with tattoos and piercings, and the like. In my righteous indignation, I fumed against and hated them. We were all wrong.

Any time we judge others, especially when we use ourselves as the standard, we step out of the path of Christ and don the garments of self-deception and hypocrisy.

This was the Pharisee's sin in the above parable. Brazenly this religious professional enters God's presence reciting his own spiritual accomplishments in comparison to the tax collector standing nearby. The Pharisee isn't praying. He is gazing into a mirror and admiring the reflection he sees there. This is a man not in love with God but in love with himself. He has gone far above and beyond all religious requirements, and he wears his deeds like so many perfect attendance pins for all to see.

That he is contrasted against a tax collector—a traitor, an untouchable, an expendable member of a class so far beneath him the distance is almost infinite—well, this makes the Pharisee look all the better. And when it comes to religion and rule keeping, looks are supremely important.

The Pharisee's conclusion is, "Thank God I am not like that."

But like what, exactly?

This is a subtle, yet deadly temptation: When Christians become known as good people, religious and respectable people, it typically means we are attractive, white, middle-class Americans who pay our bills on time, vote Republican, don't stay out past midnight, and eat lunch with the Kiwanis. It means we aren't like "that." We cheat on neither our taxes nor our spouses. We don't believe in or have abortions. We don't spend our weekends in the bars, but in the house of the Lord. We never allow anything secular to cross our children's virgin ears, and we know if Jesus were here today, he would agree with our biblical interpretations and love the church we attend.

Not so secretly, we position ourselves on the high and mighty throne of morality. Our religious zeal, and our success with it, empowers us to look down on those whose lifestyles and choices leave much to be desired, not just by us, mind you, but also by God.

With this parable, Jesus may have been taking a shot at a popular rabbinical prayer of his day. Pharisees routinely prayed:

> I thank thee, O Lord, my God, that thou hast given me a place among those who sit in the House of Study, and not among those who sit at the street corners; for I rise early and they rise early, but I rise early to study the words of the Law, and they rise early to engage in vain things; I labor and they labor, but I labor and receive a reward, and they labor and receive no reward; I live and they live, but I live for the life of the future world, and they live for the pit of destruction.[2]

The pride of the Pharisee is alive and well in the hearts and propaganda of many Christians today. That prayer sounds a lot like some of the pastoral prayers uttered in pulpits, on radios, and on evangelical cable shows across the land. "Jesus loves me, this I know, but I am certain you are going to hell."

Meanwhile, the tax collector will not even lift his head toward heaven. Rightfully, he stands at a distance, far from the altar and far from God, where he feels he belongs. Truthfully, he is everything the Pharisee says about him and worse. We have catalogued the sins of the tax collectors already, and we know these men were crooked to the core. This man is no exception and cannot be defended. He recognizes this about himself, as he looks into his own mirror, and he beats his breast, punishing his heart and body in shame. He concludes that if the dictionary had a definition for "sinner," his picture would be framed there. He can only cry out, "*Kyrie Eliason.*"

Lord, have mercy.

And again the blow from Jesus: "I tell you, this sinner, not the Pharisee, returned home justified before God" (v. 14).

Justification is a big deal in the Christian cosmos, especially to Protestants. And it should be. From the Apostle Paul to the Reformers down to the present day, the question is asked, "How is a person made right, or just, with God?" "Justification" is the one-word answer. This was certainly Paul's favorite answer. Drawing scenes from the Hebrew courts of law, Paul explained justification as an action whereby a judge ruled in favor of one party over another. A "justified" person was one determined to be found right by the court. Pauline theology is clear: God has justified sinners through the death and resurrection of Christ. He has made humankind "right."

In the zeal to recover a Pauline understanding of the gospel and avoid the works-dominated sacramental system of Catholicism, many Protestant preachers and commentators seek to make the doctrine of justification the dominating feature of the New Testament, including this parable here. This is a mistake.

Justification, with its hard and fast legalese, seems to have more followers than Jesus these days. But we are not saved by justification by faith, though such a statement is in conflict with many a sermon. No, we are saved by Jesus, by his grace and goodness. "Justification" is a handle on the theological suitcase, a fallible description, a pointer toward what Jesus has done for us. Justification is just one of a myriad of different ways to grapple with the work of Christ. The *doctrine* of justification does not dominate the New Testament, but the *fact* of justification and its implications do. And the facts are clear: "God's grace and truth came through Jesus Christ" (John 1:17), and that grace fills those who are empty of themselves.

This is the sin and sainthood of the two men in this story. One is full of himself, making it impossible for grace to fill his being, and the other is such a wreck that he has nothing left to offer but a hollow shell. God fills that vacuum with his grace. That emptiness and nothingness is the beginning of being just and made alive in Christ.

God goes where there is empty space. The objective then of the truly spiritual, Christ-following life is emptiness. It is the relinquishment of ego, pride, self-confidence, and selfishness. The challenge of living the Christian life is not the challenges that are "out there" somewhere, but the inborn self-determination of the human heart, the evil inside us all. Most of us must admit that if outer temptation did not exist, and there was no such thing as enticement or the devil to pull on our shirt tale on occasion, we would still have our hands full dealing with ourselves.

So we must seek nothing except surrender to the person of Christ and the grace of God in our lives. That is the free-falling edge Christ seeks to push us over. That is the never-ending journey we are called to follow. It is not about "trying harder" or "doing better." It is about "giving up" and acknowledging our own powerlessness.

As an example, I will remind you of a Tom Clancy-style rescue that took place in the summer of 2008. A group of fifteen hostages were rescued from Marxist rebels in the country of Columbia. The group included three Americans, high-profile politicians, and some who had been held captive for ten years. The fascinating thing was how the Columbian army pulled it off. Not a single bullet was fired, and not a single drop of blood was shed.

A disgruntled and revenge-oriented member of the rebels' senior leadership, a man trusted by the high command, agreed to cooperate. He appealed to his superiors that the hostages should be moved to a rallying point in southern Colombia, so they agreed. Then a day before the operation, two helicopters—painted white and disguised as those of a non-governmental organization—left a military base in the Andes Mountains and settled in a wilderness valley clearing. On board one of the helicopters, the one that would rescue the hostages, were four air force crew disguised as civilians, seven military intelligence agents, and the rebel turncoat. All had taken two weeks of acting lessons to appear convincing.

Once the aircraft was airborne, the rescuers swiftly overpowered the two rebels escorting the hostages, and the liberated captives celebrated so enthusiastically that the helicopter had trouble remaining in the sky.

Beyond the spy games and acting lessons, here is the real secret to the mission's success: the hostages, who unknown to them were not being transported but rescued, were tied and handcuffed when they got on the helicopter. Why? Their rescuers did not want to take the risk of the hostages attempting to save themselves and incidentally killing them all. The greatest danger to the success of the mission was not the rebels. The greatest danger was the possibility that the hostages would trust in their own abilities and attempt to save themselves and in the process scuttle the attempt of their saviors.

Religion is no different. It is an effort at self-rescue. It appeals to our inner strength and our own deluded sense of independence. It is nothing more than a corporate expression of pride and original sin. It is death.

What is sin, actually? Breaking the law? Disobeying God? Falling short of God's intentions and ideals? Sure, all of these are correct definitions. But if we go back to the Garden of Eden, back to the beginning, what violation did Adam and Eve commit? They ate a piece of low-hanging fruit off a tree.

In and of itself, that was of no consequence. It was the command of prohibition that made the act sinful. And why did God make this prohibition? Remember the name of the tree and that question is answered: it was the "tree of the knowledge of good and evil."

The Creator was the only one qualified to determine right and wrong for his creation. He called that creation, including Adam and Eve in the Genesis account, to live their lives in trustful dependence upon him. But our ancestors, and every human being since, made this fateful decision: "*I* will determine what is good and evil. *I* will choose what is right and what is wrong for me. *I* will assert my rights and my abilities to decide my own path. *I* don't need any outside authority—not even God, not even my Maker—telling me what to do with my life. *I* will take this knowledge and responsibility as my own."

Call it original sin. Call it rebellion. Call it what you will. In the end it is a declaration of independence from the One who made us and calls us into relationship with him. Original sin is nothing more than our stubborn persistence to master our fate and captain our own souls. The end result is we get what we want: our own way, self-rule, freedom to choose our own path, but at destructive cost.

The way back to the innocence of Eden is not religion, Christian or otherwise. It is surrender. It is giving back to God the knowledge of good and evil. It is saying to him, "I cannot decide what is best for me or for your world. I cannot live out what is best for me and your world. I surrender."

Kyrie Eliason.

Lord, have mercy.

This is why it sometimes feels so disorienting to follow Jesus. This is why we cling with white knuckles and scraping fingernails to the religious lives we lead. Everything in our human nature screams out, "Take charge of your life. Make your own decisions. Pull yourself up by your own bootstraps. Protect yourself and your interests. Never give up your control. Don't let anybody else tell you what to do." And religion is used as a prideful tool of this kind of selfishness, not pointing us to a freefall into the grace of the God, but to a false sense of being right, reinforcing the self-damning pride of original sin. Religion tricks us into putting confidence in ourselves and not God's grace. It leads us deeper into original sin and away from following Jesus.

While in college I went with a friend to a revival in the town of Hollywood, Georgia. That's right, there is such a place: Hollywood, Georgia.

"On a clear night you can see all the stars," the locals say (go ahead and groan). This revival was the typical Southern affair. The Baptist church had secured the services of a big-name evangelist, faithful church members had packed the pews to capacity, and there was the eager anticipation of souls flooding the altars at the time of invitation.

As I made my way to the front door, I passed a long line of Harley Davidson motorcycles. These were not the Baby Boomer playthings so many graying men and women ride today as a hobby or youthful escape. These were hardcore, gang-style cycles. And just inside the church, there on the back pew, lo and behold, the gang sat. Leather, studs, rippling arms, ponytails, tattoos: it was the complete Hell's Angels package, sitting in a Baptist church in Hollywood, Georgia.

You can guess what my first reaction was. I said to myself, and then to my friend, "Good. Maybe these heathens will get saved tonight." And I meant it. I sat several pews away from them and found myself piously praying for their salvation because I just knew they were seconds from splitting hell wide open.

After the service got started, the pastor called on one of the deacons of the church to come forward and offer a prayer and word of introduction. One of those wicked bikers rose from his seat and started down the aisle. At first I thought the call of his bladder had merely coincided with the pastor's invitation. And being a biker and all, I was certain he was short on manners and he did not know that prayer time was an inappropriate moment to visit the latrine. When the big mountain of a man turned for the pulpit, my pulse quickened as I thought he was going forward to cause a disturbance.

He caused a disturbance, all right, but not like I thought. This chaps-wearing biker with a beard to his waist was the aforementioned deacon.

I found out later that this biker-deacon was a self-financed missionary to the roadhouses, biker bars, strip clubs, and truck stops of America. Up and down the highways with his fellow laborers—his motorcycle gang—he rode his horse of steel and entered places where good Christian people would never be caught, not even to share the gospel. He went to places where people drank too much, showed too much skin, engaged in too much sensuality, and waged too much violence. But there he shared Jesus, led Bible studies, prayed for those who thought they didn't have a prayer left, and even baptized a few souls in the truck-stop showers when necessary.

I left that Hollywood church thinking it would have been better to give the revival budget to this biker's ministry rather than spending it on some flamboyant evangelist with a bouffant hairdo and expensive cuff links. And certainly I left with a lesson scorched deep in my conscience: Never point a finger or a prayer at those you consider sinners. They may be more holy than you can imagine.

Who is it that you look down upon? Who do you compare yourself to in prayer? The liberal? The homosexual? The Bible thumper preaching on the street? The fundamentalist? The addict? Religion convinces its adherents that they are right, that they are better than others, especially these others who are so beneath them.

Religion is an understated but just as deadly form of self-centeredness. It is a fig leaf for those who choose to hide and distance themselves from the God who only wants his children to journey with him through the garden of his creation.

Lord, have mercy.

Notes

1. Dorothy Sayers as quoted by Philip Yancey, *Disappointment with God*, (Grand Rapids: Zondervan, 1992), 147.

2. George Arthur Buttrick and S. MacLean Gilmour, *The Interpreter's Bible*, vol. 8 (Nashville: Abingdon Press, 1987), 308.

Reflection Questions

1. I describe the "creep" process in this chapter. How has your life with Christ bent you in a direction you would not have chosen?

2. Why does it feel good to criticize others, especially those we deem beneath us?

3. I say in this chapter that it is a mistake to view the doctrine of justification as the "dominating feature of the New Testament." Explain why you agree or disagree with this statement.

4. Which is more difficult for you: temptation on the outside or temptation from within? Why?

5. I conclude that religion is a fig leaf we use to hide from God. Do you agree or disagree?

____

____

____

____

____

Conclusion

> Up on your feet. A long road and hard climbing lie ahead.
>
> —Virgil to Dante in the *Inferno*

Tony Soprano sits in a little diner with his family. Carmela, Meadow, AJ; they are all there, together, safe and sound. The jukebox plays a great 1980s tune by the band Journey, "Don't Stop Believing."

Meanwhile, Tony looks over his shoulder, suspicious of the movement of the other diner patrons and more than a little paranoid. The hunch is that Tony Soprano is finally going to get what is coming to him. Someone else in the diner may attempt to whack him at any moment. That is what I and twelve million other viewers expected in the final act of *The Sopranos* television series: a "badda-bing-badda-boom" conclusion, a nicely packaged finale where, after nearly ninety episodes, everything is resolved. But that is not what we got at all.

The bell jingles at the diner's door. Tony Soprano looks up, and the screen goes gray.

Millions of us scrambled for our remote controls or cursed our cable company before realizing that we had been had. Director David Chase had made his point brilliantly. The Soprano family is moving on. Their journey continues even though we will not be a part of it. Their conclusion is left to our imagination.

The writer of Luke's Gospel beat Chase to the punch by a few years. The Great Journey of Jesus, the journey that consumes so much of Luke's writings and that has consumed your time in reading this book, is never resolved. Luke does not lead Jesus triumphantly into Jerusalem as we expect, at least not yet. Jesus wanders back along the dusty roads of Judea, and we are left with the gray screen and white noise of a not-so-concluding conclusion.

Why? Because Luke knows the journey of following Jesus never ends. The freefall into his grace has no bottom. While arrogant religionists and the systems that so frequently eclipse our Lord's simple call to discipleship will one day pass away, the pursuit of Christ will not. The follower of Jesus must take his or her never-ending journey to its own conclusion, for such is the life of adventuresome discipleship.

On the last night of his own earthly journey, Jesus turned to his blessed but dim-witted disciples and asked, "Have I been with you all this time, and yet you still don't know who I am?"

I am afraid we are no different from those first disciples, for the answer is still, "no." There are days we must admit we do not recognize him, for just when we think we have him figured out, he does something crazy. He commands us to love our enemies; he tells us to do good to those who do not deserve it; he challenges us to give away our possessions; he says we should turn the other cheek or be crucified alongside him.

In his eccentric, revolutionary way, Jesus runs roughshod over our preconceptions. He overturns the established order of our lives. He surprises us with his grace. He calls us to himself, demanding our souls, our lives, our all. This is why we follow Jesus of Nazareth, known and unknown, revealed and hidden, resisted and loved, for only he holds the very words and way of life.

I do not know where Jesus will lead you. I have no idea of the long journey that waits for any of us. But I do know it begins with that first step; that first halting, timid step that puts you on the road away from religion and onward to the Christ. When we get to the finish, we will begin together anew an eternity-long exploration of this One who always calls us to follow him.

You have got a long way to go, so take care of yourself. Stop and rest when you must. Do a little sightseeing along the way. Let others help you. And never forget that while the road is long, the One we follow is very much worth it.

Take courage for your journey with these words from *The Book of Common Prayer*:

> O God, our heavenly Father, whose glory fills the whole creation, and whose presence we find wherever we go: Preserve those who travel; surround them with your loving care; protect them from every danger; and bring them in safety to their journey's end; through Jesus Christ our Lord.
>
> *Amen.*